William Hepworth Dixon

**New America**

Volume II.

William Hepworth Dixon

**New America**
*Volume II.*

ISBN/EAN: 9783741178948

Manufactured in Europe, USA, Canada, Australia, Japa

Cover: Foto ©Andreas Hilbeck / pixelio.de

Manufactured and distributed by brebook publishing software (www.brebook.com)

William Hepworth Dixon

**New America**

# COLLECTION
## OF
# BRITISH AUTHORS.
### VOL. 929.

NEW AMERICA BY W. H. DIXON.

IN TWO VOLUMES.
VOL. II.

# NEW AMERICA.

BY

WILLIAM HEPWORTH DIXON,

AUTHOR OF "THE HOLY LAND," ETC.

COPYRIGHT EDITION.

IN TWO VOLUMES

VOL. II.

LEIPZIG

BERNHARD TAUCHNITZ

1867.

# CONTENTS

## OF VOLUME II.

|  |  |  | Page |
|---|---|---|---|
| CHAPTER | I. | Uncle Sam's Estate | 7 |
| — | II. | The Four Races | 14 |
| — | III. | Sex and Sex | 22 |
| — | IV. | Ladies | 31 |
| — | V. | Squatter Women | 38 |
| — | VI. | Feminine Politics | 45 |
| — | VII. | Husbands and Wives | 54 |
| — | VIII. | Domestic Law | 60 |
| — | IX. | Mount Lebanon | 69 |
| — | X. | A Shaker House | 77 |
| — | XI. | Shaker Union | 86 |
| — | XII. | Mother Ann | 95 |
| — | XIII. | Resurrection Order | 105 |
| — | XIV. | Spiritual Cycles | 114 |
| — | XV. | Spiritualism | 123 |
| — | XVI. | Female Seers | 137 |
| — | XVII. | Equal Rights | 144 |
| — | XVIII. | The Harmless People | 151 |
| — | XIX. | The Revolt of Woman | 160 |
| — | XX. | Oneida Creek | 171 |

## CONTENTS OF VOLUME II.

| | Page |
|---|---|
| CHAPTER XXI. Holiness | 180 |
| — XXII. A Bible Family | 188 |
| — XXIII. New Foundations | 199 |
| — XXIV. Pantagamy | 208 |
| — XXV. Young America | 218 |
| — XXVI. Manners | 223 |
| — XXVII. Liberties | 232 |
| — XXVIII. Law and Justice | 239 |
| — XXIX. Politics | 246 |
| — XXX. North and South | 256 |
| — XXXI. Colour | 265 |
| — XXXII. Reconstruction | 276 |
| — XXXIII. Union | 287 |

# NEW AMERICA.

## CHAPTER I.

#### Uncle Sam's Estate.

In climbing the slopes of yon rivers from New York to Toledo; in running down the Mississippi Valley from Toledo to St. Louis; in mounting the Prairies from St. Louis to Virginia Dale; in crossing the Sierras from Virginia Dale to the Great Salt Lake; in winding through the Wasatch chain, the Bitter-creek country, and the Plains from Salt Lake City to Omaha; in descending the Missouri from the middle waters to its mouth; in traversing the table-lands of Indiana and Ohio; in threading the mountain-passes of Pennsylvania; in piercing the forests, following the streams, lounging in the cities of Virginia; in pacing these streets of Washington, mixing with these people in the gardens of the White House, and under the dome of the Capitol, a man will find himself growing free of many great facts. He will be in daily contact with the newest forms of life, with a world in the earlier stages of its growth, with a society everywhere young in genius, enterprise, and virtue; but probably no other fact will strike his imagination with so large a force as the size of what is here called, in the idiom of the people, Uncle Sam's Estate.

"Sir," said to me a Minnesota farmer, "the curse of this country is that we have too much land;" a phrase which I have heard again and again; among the iron-masters of Pittsburgh, among the tobacco-planters of Richmond, among the cotton-spinners of Worcester. Indeed, this wail against the land is common among men who, having mines, plantations, mills, and farms, would like to have large supplies of labour at lower rates of wages than the market yields. There have been times in which a similar cry was raised in England, by the Norfolk farmers, by the Manchester spinners, by the Newcastle coalmen. Those who want to get labour on the lowest terms must always be in favour of restricting the productive acreage of land. But whether a Minnesota farmer, a Pennsylvania miner, or a Massachusetts cotton-spinner, may like it or dislike it, nobody can dispute the fact that the first impression stamped on a traveller's eye and brain in this great country is that of stupendous size.

During the Civil War, when the Trent affair was waxing warm between the two main branches of our race — a brothers' quarrel, in which there was some right and a little wrong on both sides — a New York publisher put out a map of the United States and Territories, stretching from the Atlantic Ocean to the Pacific Ocean, from the line of the great lakes to the gulfs of Mexico and California, on the margin of which map there was an outline of England drawn to scale. Perhaps it had not been designed by the draughtsman to rebuke our pride; still, it made us look very small on paper; and if we had been a people piquing ourselves on the possession of "much dirt" in the Home County called England, that map might have cut us to the quick. Space is not one of our island points. In three or four hours we hurry from sea to sea, from Liverpool to Hull, from the Severn to the Thames; in the lapse between breakfast and dinner we wing our way from London to York, from Manchester to Norwich, from Oxford to Penzance. It is the common joke of New York, that a Yankee in London dares not leave his hotel after dark lest he should slip off the foreland and be drowned in the sea.

The Republic owns within her two ocean frontiers more than three million square miles of land; a fourth part of a million square miles of water, either salt or fresh; a range of Alps, a range of Pyrenees, a range of Apennines; forests by the side of which the Schwarzwald and the Ardennes would be German toys; rivers exceeding the Danube and the Rhine, as much as these rivers exceed the Mersey and the Clyde.

Under the crystal roof in Hyde Park, when the nations had come together in 1851, each bringing what it found to be its best and rarest to a common testing place, America was for many weeks of May and June represented by one great article — a vast, unoccupied space. An eagle spread its wings over an empty kingdom, while the neighbouring states of Belgium, Holland, Prussia, and France, were crowded like swarms of bees in their summer hives. Some persons smiled, with a mocking lip, at that paper bird, brooding in silence above a mighty waste: but I for one never came from the thronging courts of Europe into that large allotment of space and light, without feeling that our cousins of the West had hit, though it may have been by chance, on a very happy expression of their virgin wealth. In Hyde Park, as at home, they showed that they had room enough and to spare.

Yes: the Republic is a big country. In England, we have no lines of sufficient length, no areas of sufficient width, to convey a just idea of its size. Our longest line is that running from Land's End to Berwick, — a line which is some miles shorter than the distance from Washington to Lexington. Our broadest valley is that of the Thames, — the whole of which would lie hidden from sight in a corner of the Sierra Madre. The state of Oregon is bigger than England; California is about the size of Spain; Texas would be larger than France if France had won the frontier of the German Rhine. If the United States were parted into equal lots, they would make fifty-two kingdoms as large as England, fourteen empires as large as France. Even the grander figure of Europe, — the seat of our great powers, and of many lesser powers, — a continent which we used to call the world, and fight to maintain in delicate balance of parts, — fails us when we come to measure in its lines such amplitudes as those of the United States.' To wit; from Eastport to Brownsville is farther than from London to Tuat, in the Great Sahara; from Washington to Astoria is farther than from Brussels to Kars; from New York to San Francisco is farther than from Paris to Bagdad. Such measures seem to carry us away from the sphere of fact into the realms of magic and romance.

Again, take the length of rivers as a measurement of size. A steamboat can go ninety miles up the Thames; two hundred miles up the Seine; five hundred and fifty miles up the Rhine. In America, the Thames would be a creek, the Seine a brook, the Rhine a local stream, soon lost in a mightier flood. Some of these great rivers, like the Kansas and the Platte, flowing through boundless plains, are nowhere deep enough for steamers, though they are sometimes miles in width; yet the navigable length of many of these streams is a wearisome surprise. The Mississippi is five times longer than the Rhine; the Missouri is three times longer than the Danube; the Columbia is four times longer than the Scheldt. From the sea to Fort Snelling, the Mississipi is ploughed by steamers a distance of two thousand one hundred and thirty-one miles; yet she is but the second river in the United States.

Glancing at a map of America, we see to the north a group of lakes. Now, our English notion of a lake is likely to have been derived from Coniston, Killarney, Lomond, Leman, and Garda. But these sheets of water give us no true hint of what Huron and Superior are like, scarcely indeed of what Erie and Ontario are like. Coniston, Killarney, Lomond, Leman, and Garda, put together, would not cover a tenth part of the surface occupied by the smallest of the five American lakes. All the waters lying in Swiss, Italian, English, Irish, Scotch, and German lakes, might be poured into Michigan without making a perceptible addition to its flood. Yorkshire might be sunk out of sight in Erie; Ontario drowns as much land as would make two duchies equal in area to Schleswig and Holstein. Denmark proper could bo washed by the waves of Huron. Many of the minor lakes of America would be counted as inland seas elsewhere; to wit, Salt Lake, in Utah, has a surface of two thousand square miles; while that of Geneva has only three hundred and thirty; that of Como, only ninety; that of Killarney, only eight. A kingdom like Saxony, a principality like Parma, a duchy like Coburg, if thrown in one heap into Lake Superior, might add an island to its beauty, but would be no more conspicuous in its vast expanse than one of those pretty green islets which adorn Loch Lomond.

Mountain masses are not considered by some as the strongest points of American scenery; yet you find masses in this country which defy all measurement by such puny chains as the Pyrenees, the Apennines, and the Savoy Alps. The Alleghanies, ranging in height between Helvellyn and Pilatus, run through a district equal in extent to the country lying betwen Ostend and Jaroslaw. The Wasatch chain, though the name is hardly known in Europe, has a larger bulk and grandeur than the Julian Alps. The Sierra Madre, commonly called the Rocky Mountains, ranging in stature from a little below Snowdon to a trifle above Mont Blanc, extend from Mexico, through the Republic into British America, a distance almost equal to that dividing London from Delhi.

No doubt, then, can be felt as to the size of this Anglo-Saxon estate. America is a big country; and size, as we know in other things, becomes, in the long run, a measure of political power.

Leaving out of view all rivers, all lakes, there remain in the United States about one thousand nine hundred and twenty-six million acres; nearly all of them productive land; forest, prairie, down, alluvial bottom; all lying in the temperate zone; healthy in climate, rich in wood, in coal, in oil, in iron; a landed estate that could give to each head of five million families a lot of three hundred and eighty-five acres.

## CHAPTER II.

#### The Four Races.

On this fine estate of land and water dwells a strange variety of races. No society in Europe can pretend to such wide contrasts in the type, in the colour, as are here observable; for while in France, in Germany, in England, we are all white men, deriving our blood and lineage from a common Aryan stock, and having in our habits, languages, and creeds, a certain bond of brotherhood, our friends in the United States, in addition to such pale varieties as the Saxon and Celt; the Swabian and Gaul, have also the Sioux, the Negro and the Tartar; nations and tribes, not few in number, not guests of a moment, here to-day and gone to-morrow; but crowding hosts of men and women, who have the rights which come of either being born on the soil or of being settled on it for life. White men, black men, red men, yellow men; they are citizens of this country, paying its taxes, feeding on its produce, obeying its laws.

In England we are apt to boast of having fused into one strong amalgam men of the most hostile qualities of blood; blending into a perfect unit the steadfast Saxon, the volatile Celt, the splendid Norman, and the frugal Pict; but our faint distinctions of race and race fade wholly out of sight, when they are put alongside of the fierce antagonisms seen on this American soil. In the Old World we have separate classes, where in this new country they have opposite nations; we have slight variation in the quality, where they have radical difference in the type. To a negro in Georgia, to a Pawnee in Dakota, to a Chinese in Montana, a white man is just a white man; no more, no less; the Gaul, the Dane, the Spaniard, the Saxon, being, in his simple eyes, brethren of one family, members of one church. Our subtler distinctions of race and race are wholly invisible in this stranger's eyes.

In the western country you may sit down at dinner in some miner's house with a dozen guests, who shall not be matched, in contrasting types and colours, even in a Cairene bazaar, an Aleppo gateway, a Stamboul mosque. On either side of you may sit — a Polish Jew, an Italian count, a Choctaw chief, a Mexican rancher, a Confederate soldier (there called "a white-washed reb"), a Mormon bishop, a Sandwich-island sailor, a Parsee merchant, a Boston bag-man, a Missouri boss. A negro may cook your meat, a Chinese draw your cork, while the daughters of your host, — bright girls, dainty, well dressed, — may serve the dishes and pour out your wine; the whole company being drawn into these western regions by the rage for gold, and melting towards each other, more like guests who dine in a New York hotel than like strangers who come either to trade in an Egyptian bazaar, to lodge in a Syrian khan, or pray in a Turkish mosque. You may find, too, under one roof as many creeds as colours. Your host may be a Universalist; one of that soft American sect which holds that nobody on earth will ever be damned, though the generous and illogical fellow can hardly open his lips without calling on one of his guests to be so. The Mormon will put his trust in Joseph, as a natural seer and revelator: the Chinese will worship Buddha, of whom he knows nothing but the name; the Jew will pray to Jehovah, of whom he cannot be said to know much more. The Choctaw chief may invoke the Big Father, whom white men call for him the Great Spirit. Sam — all negroes there are Sams — may be a Methodist; an Episcopal Methodist, mind you; Sam and his sable brethren hating everything that is low. The Italian count is an infidel; the Mexican a Catholic. Your white-washed reb, repudiating all religions, gives his mind to cock-tails. The Missourian is a Come-outer, a member of one of those new churches of America which profess to have brought God nearer to the earth. That the Parsee holds a private opinion about the sun we may fairly guess; Queen Emma's countryman is a Pagan; while the Boston bag-man, now a Calvinist, damning the company to future miseries of fire and brimstone, was once a Communist of the school of Noyes.

White men, black men, red men, yellow men, — all these chief types and colours of the human race, — have been drawn into company on this western soil, this middle continent, lying between China and the Archipelago on one side, Africa and Europe on the other, where they crowd and contest the ground under a common flag.

The White Man, caring for neither frost nor fire, so long as he can win good food for his mouth, fit clothing for his limbs, appears to be the master in every zone; able to endure all climates, to undertake all labours, to overcome all trials, casting nets into the Bay of Fundy, cradling gold in the Sacramento valleys, raising dates and lemons in Florida, trapping beavers in Oregon, raising herds of kine in Texas, spinning thread in Massachusetts, clearing woods in Kansas, smelting iron in Pennsylvania, talking buncombe in Columbia, writing leaders in New York. He is the man of plastic genius, of enduring character; equally at home among the palm-trees and the pines; in every latitude the guide, the employer, and the king of all.

The Black Man, a true child of the tropics, to whom warmth is like the breath of life, flees from those bleak fields of the north, in which the white man repairs his fibre and renews his blood; preferring the swamps and savannahs of the south, where, among palms, cotton-plants, and sugar-canes, he finds the rich colours in which his eye delights, the sunny heats in which his blood expands. Freedom would not tempt him to go northward into frost and fog. Even now, when Massachusetts and Connecticut tempt him by the offer of good wages, easy work, and sympathising people, he will not go to them. He only just endures New York; the most hardy of his race will hardly stay in Saratoga and Niagara beyond the summer months. Since the South has been made free for Sam to live in, he has turned his back on the cold and friendly North, in search of a brighter home. Sitting in the ricefield, by the cane-brake, under the mulberry-trees of his darling Alabama, with his kerchief round his head, his banjo on his knee, he is joyous as a bird, singing his endless and foolish roundelay, and feeling the sunshine burn upon his face. The negro is but a local fact in the country; having his proper home in a corner — the most sunny corner — of the United States.

The Red Man, once a hunter of the Alleghanies, not less than of the prairies and the Rocky Mountains, has been driven by the pale-face, he and his squaw, his elk, his buffalo, and his antelope, into the far Western country; into the waste and desolate lands lying westward of the Mississippi and Missouri. The exceptions hardly break the rule. A band of picturesque pedlars may be found at Niagara; Red Jackets, Cherokee chiefs, and Mohawks; selling bows and canes, and generally spunging on those youths and damsels who roam about the Falls in search of opportunities to flirt. A colony, hardly of a better sort, may be found at Oneida Creek, in Madison county; the few sowing maize, growing fruit, and singing psalms; the many starving on the soil, cutting down the oak and maple, alienating the best acres, pining after their brethren who have thrown the white man's gift in his face, and gone away with their weapons and their war-paint. Red Jacket at the Falls, Bill Beechtree at Oneida Creek — the first selling beaded work to girls, the second twisting hickory canes for boys — are the last representatives of mighty nations, hunters and warriors, who at one time owned the broad lands from the Susquehannah to Lake Erie. Red Jacket will not settle; Bill Beechtree is incapable of work. The red-skin will not dig, and to beg he is not ashamed. Hence, he has been pushed away from his place, driven out by the spade, and kept at bay by the smoke of chimney fires. A wild man of the plain and forest, he makes his home with the wolf, the rattle-snake, the buffalo, and the elk. When the wild beast flies, the wild man follows. The Alleghany slopes, on which, only seventy years ago, he chased the elk and scalped the white woman, will hear his war-whoop, see his war-dance, feel his scalping knife, no more. In the western country he is still a figure in the landscape. From the Missouri to the Colorado he is master of all the open plains; the forts which the white men have built to protect their roads to San Francisco, like the Turkish block-houses built along the Syrian tracks, being mainly of use as a hint of their great reserve of power. The red men find it hard to lay down a tomahawk, to take up a hoe; some thousands only of them have yet done so; some hundreds only have learned from the whites to drink gin and bitters, to lodge in frame-houses, to tear up the soil, to forget the chase, the war-dance, and the Great Spirit.

The Yellow Man, generally a Chinese, often a Malay, sometimes a Dyak, has been drawn into the Pacific states from Asia, and from the Eastern Archipelago, by the hot demand for labour; any kind of which comes to him as a boon. From digging in the mine to cooking an omelette and ironing a shirt, he is equal to everything by which dollars can be gained. Of these yellow people there are now sixty thousand in California, Utah, and Montana; they come and go; but many more of them come than go. As yet these harmless crowds are weak and useful. Hop Chang keeps a laundry; Chi Hi goes out as cook; Cum Thing is a maid-of-all-work. They are in no man's way, and they labour for a crust of bread; carrying the hod when Mike has run away to the diggings, and scrubbing the floor when Biddy has made some wretch the happiest of his sex. Supple and patient, these yellow men, though far from strong, are eager for any kind of work; but they prefer the employments of women to those of men; delighting in an engagement to wash clothes, to nurse babies, and to wait on guests. They make very good butlers and chamber-maids. Loo Sing, a jolly old girl in pig-tail, washes your shirts, starching and ironing them very neatly, except that you cannot persuade him to refrain from spitting on your cuffs and fronts. To him spitting on linen is the same as damping it with drops of water; and the habits of his life prevent him, even though you should catch him by the pig-tail, and rub his tiny bit of nose on the burning iron, from seeing that it is not the same to you. To-day, those yellow men are sixty thousand weak; in a few years they may be six hundred thousand strong. They will ask for votes. They will hold the balance of parties. In some districts they will make a majority; selecting the judges, forming the juries, interpreting the laws. Those yellow men are Buddhists, professing polygamy, practising infanticide.

Next year is not more sure to come in its own season, than a great society of Asiatics to dwell on the Pacific slopes. A Buddhist church, fronting the Buddhist churches in China and Ceylon, will rise in California, Oregon, and Nevada. More than all, a war of labour will commence between the races which feed on beef and the races which thrive on rice; one of those wars in which the victory is not necessarily with the strong.

White man, black man, red man, yellow man, each has a custom of his own to follow, a genius of his own to prove, a conscience of his own to respect; custom which is not of kin, genius which is largely different, and conscience which is fiercely hostile. These four great types might be represented to the eye by four of my friends; H. W. Longfellow, poet, Boston; Eli Brown, waiter, Richmond; Spotted Dog, savage, Rocky Mountains; and Loo Sing, laundry boy, Nevada. Under what circumstances will they blend into a common stock?

## CHAPTER III.

#### Sex and Sex.

Next, perhaps, after its huge size, and its varied races, the fact which is apt to strike a stranger most in the United States, is the disproportion almost everywhere to be noted between sex and sex.

To such a dinner as we have imagined taking place in the western country, no woman will have sat down; not because there are no ladies in the house, but because those ladies have something else to do than dine with guests. Your host may have been a married man, pluming himself with very good right, on his winsome wife, his bevy of sparkling girls; but his wife and her daughters, instead of occupying seats at the board, will have to stand behind the chairs, handing round the dishes, pouring out the tea, aiding Loo Sing to uncork the wine. Females are few in yonder western towns; you may spend day after day without falling in sight of a pretty face. At the wayside inn, when you call for the chamber-maid, either Sam puts in his woolly head, or Chi Hi pops in his shaven crown. Hardly any help can be hired in those wastes; Molly runs away with a miner; Biddy gets married to a merchant; and when guests ride in from the track, the fair creatures who live on the spot, the joy of some husband's home, of some father's eyes, have no choice beyond either sending these guests on their way, hungry, unrested, or cooking them a dinner and putting it on the board. At Salt Lake, in the houses of Mormon apostles and of wealthy merchants, we were always served by the young ladies, often by extremely delicate and lovely girls.

At first this novelty is rather hard to bear; not by the ladies so much as by their guests. To see a woman who has just been quoting Keats and playing Gounod, standing up behind your seat, uncorking catawba, whipping away plates, and handing you the sauce, is trying to the nerves, especially when you are young and passably polite. In time you get used to it, as you do to the sight of a scalping-knife, to the sound of a war-whoop; but what can a lady at the mines, on the prairies, on the lonely farmsteads, do when a guest drops in? Help she has none, excepting Sam and Loo Sing. In that district of many males and few females, every girl is a lady, almost every woman is a wife. Men may be hired at a fair day's wage, to do any kind of male labour; to cook your food, to groom your horse, to trim your garden, to cut your wood; but women to do female work, to make the beds, to serve at table, to nurse the bairns; no, not for the income of a bishop, can you get them. Biddy can do better. Girls who are young and pretty have a lottery full of prizes ready to their hand; even those who may be old and plain can have husbands when they please. Everywhere west of the Mississippi there is a brisk demand for women; and what girl of spirit would let herself out for hire, when the church door is open, and the bridal bells are ready? Who would accept the position of a woman's help, when she has only to say the word, and become a man's helpmate?

Your hostess on the Plains may have been well born, well educated, well dressed; both she herself and her bevy of girls may be such as would be considered magnetic in Fifth Avenue, attractive in May Fair. They may speak French very well; and when some of you selfish fellows gathered under their window to smoke and chat, they will have charmed your ears with the most brilliant passages from Faust. Now, to hear Siebel's serenade in the shadow of the Rocky Mountains is a treat on which you may not have counted; but the fact remains that only one hour earlier in the day the contralto has been acting as your cook. Once before in my life the same sort of thing has occurred to me; in Morocco, where a dark-eyed Judith, daughter of a Jew in whose house I was lodging for the night, first fried my supper of fowls and tomatoes, and then lulled me to sleep by the notes of her guitar, as she sat on the door-step.

This comedy of the sexes may be found in action, not only out yonder in Colorado and the western prairies, but here in the shadow of the Capitol, in every State of the Union, almost in every city of each State. After all the havoc of war — of which this disparity between males and females was an active, though an unseen, cause — the evidence of inequality meets you at every turn; in the ball-rooms at Washington, in the streets of New York, in the chapels of Boston, at the dinner-tables of

Richmond, as well as among the frame sheds of Omaha, in the plantations of Atlanta, in the miner's huts near Denver, in the theatre of Salt Lake City. The cry is everywhere for girls; girls, — more girls! In a hundred voices you hear the echoes of a common want; the ladies cannot find servants, the dancers cannot get partners, the young men cannot win wives. I was at a ball on the Missouri river, where half the men had to sit down, though the girls obligingly danced every set.

Compared against the society of Paris and of London, that of America seems to be all awry. Go into the Madeleine, — it is full of ladies; go into St. James's Palace, — it is full of ladies. Every house in England has excess of daughters, about whom mothers have their little dreams, not always unmixed with a little fear. When Blanche is thirty, and still unsettled, her very father must begin to doubt of her ever going out into life. An old adage runs, that a girl at twenty says to herself, Who will suit me? at thirty, Whom shall I suit? Here in America it is not the woman, but the man, who is a drug in the matrimonial market. No Yankee girl is bound, like a Scottish lassie, like an Irish kerne, to serve in another woman's house for bread. Her face is her fortune and her lips a prize; her love more precious than her labour; her two bright orbs of more value than even her nimble hands. War may have thinned to her disadvantage the rank and file of lovers; but the losses of male life by shot and shell, by fever and ague, by waste and privation, have been more than replaced to her from Europe;

and the disproportions of sex and sex, noted before the war broke out, are said to be greater since its close. The lists are crowded with bachelors wanting wives; the price of young men is ruling down; and only the handsome, well-doing fellows have a chance of going off!

This sketch is no effort of a fancy, looking for extremes and loving the grotesque. When the census was compiled (in 1860), the white males were found to be in excess of the white females, by seven hundred and thirty thousand souls. Such a fact has no fellow in Europe, except in the Papal States, where society is made by exceptional forces, governed by exceptional rules. In every other Christian country, — in France, England, Germany, Spain, — the females are in large excess of the males. In France there are two hundred thousand women more than men; in England three hundred and sixty-five thousand. The unusual rule here noticed in America is not confined to any district, any sea-board, any zone. Out of forty-six organised States and Territories, only eight exhibit the ordinary rule of European countries. Eight old settlements are supplied with women; that is to say, Maryland, Massachusetts, New Hampshire, New Jersey, New York, North Carolina, Rhode Island, Columbia; while the other thirty-eight settlements, purchases, and conquests, from the Atlantic Ocean to the Pacific Ocean, lack this element of a stable, orderly, and virtuous state, — a wife for every young man of a proper age to marry. In some of the western regions, the disparity is such as strikes the moralist with awe: in

California there are three men to every woman; in Washington, four men to every woman; in Nevada, eight men to every woman; in Colorado, twenty men to every woman.

This disparity between sex and sex is not wholly caused, as will be thought, by the large immigration of single men. It is so in degree, no doubt, since far more males arrive by ship at Boston and New York than females; but if all the new comers were sent back, if no fresh male were allowed to land in New York unless he brought with him a female companion, a sister, a wife, still a large percentage of the people would have to go down into their graves unmarried. More males are born than females. Casting off the German and Irish quota, there would still be four men in the hundred in this great Republic for whom nature has sent no female mates. Immigration only comes to the help of nature; Europe sending in hosts of bachelors to fight for the few women, who would otherwise be insufficient for the native men. In the whole mass of whites, the disproportion is five in the hundred; so that one man in every twenty males born in the United States can never expect to have a wife of his own.

What is hardly less strange than this large displacement of the sexes among the white population, is the fact that it is not explained and corrected by any excess in the inferior types. There are more yellow men than yellow women, more red braves than red squaws. Only the negroes are of nearly equal number; a slight excess being counted on the female side.

Very few Tartars and Chinese have brought their wives and daughters with them into this country. On their first coming over they expected to get rich in a year, and return to sip tea and grow oranges in their native land. Many of those who are now settled in California and Montana, are sending for their mates, who may come or not; having mostly, perhaps, been married again in the absence of their lords. The present rate is eighteen yellow men to one yellow woman.

As yet, the red-skins have been counted in groups and patches only; in the more settled districts of Michigan, Minnesota, California, and New Mexico; but in all these districts, though the influences are here unusually favourable to female life, males are found in excess of females, in the proportion of five to four.

Think what this large excess of men over women entails, in the way of trial, on American society — think what a state that country must be in which counts up in its fields, in its cities, seven hundred and thirty thousand unmarried men!

Bear in mind that these crowds of prosperous fellows are not bachelors by choice, selfish dogs, woman-haters, men useless to themselves and to the world in which they live. They are average young men, busy and pushing; fellows who would rather fall into love than into sin; who would be fond of their wives and proud of their children if society would only provide them with lawful mates. What are they now? An army of monks without the defence of a religious vow. These seven hundred and thirty thousand bachelors have never promised to be chaste; many of them, it may be feared, regard the tenth commandment as little more than a paper law. You say to them in effect, "You are not to pluck these flowers, not to trample on these borders, if you please." Suppose that they will not please? How is the unwedded youth to be hindered from coveting his neighbour's wife? You know what Naples is, what Munich is. You have seen the condition of Liverpool, Cadiz, Antwerp, Livorno; of every city, of every port, in which there is a floating population of single men; but in which of these cities do you find any approach to New York, in the show of open and triumphant vice?

Men who know New York far worse than myself, assure me that in depth and darkness of iniquity, neither Paris in its private haunts, nor London in its open streets, can hold a candle to it. Paris may be subtler, London may be grosser, in its vices; but for largeness of depravity, for domineering insolence of sin, for rowdy callousness to censure, they tell me the Atlantic city finds no rival on the earth.

Do all these evils come with the anchoring ship, and stream from the quays into the city? No one will say so. The quays of New York are like the quays of any other port. They are the haunts of drabs and thieves; they are covered with grog-shops and stews; but the men who land on those quays are not viler in taste than those who land in Southampton, in Hamburg, in Genoa. What, then, makes the Empire City a cesspool by the side of which European ports seem almost pure? My answer is, mainly the disparity of sex and sex.

New York is a great capital; rich and pleasant, gay and luxurious; a city of freedom, a city of pleasure, to which men come from every part of the Union; this man for trade, that for counsel, a third for relaxation, a fourth for adventure. It is a place for the idle man, as well as for the busy man. Crowds flock to its hotels, to its theatres, to its gaming-houses; and we need no angel from heaven to tell us what kind of company will amuse an unmarried man having dollars in his purse.

On the other side, this demand for mates who can never be supplied, not in one place only, but in every place alike, affects the female mind with a variety of plagues; driving your sister into a thousand restless agitations about her rights and powers; into debating woman's era in history, woman's place in creation, woman's mission in the family; into public hysteria, into table-rapping, into anti-wedlock societies, into theories about free love, natural marriage, and artistic maternity; into anti-offspring resolutions, into sectarian polygamy, into free trade of the affections, into community of wives. Some part of this wild disturbance of the female mind, it may be urged, is due to the freedom and prosperity which women find in America as compared against what they enjoy in Europe; but this freedom, this prosperity, are in some degree, at least, the consequences of that disparity in numbers which makes the hand of every young girl in the United States a positive prize.

## CHAPTER IV.

### Ladies.

"The American lady has not made an American home," says sly old Mayo; a truth which I should hardly have found out, had I not met with it in an American author. Ladies, it is true, are very much at home in hotels; but I have only to remember certain streets in Boston, Philadelphia, Richmond, and New York — indeed, in Denver, Salt Lake City, and St. Louis — to feel that America has homes as bright as any to be found in Middlesex and Kent. "What do you say, now, to our ladies?" enquired a bluff Yankee; as we sat last night under the verandah, here in the hotel at Saratoga. "Charming," of course I answered, "pale, delicate, bewitching." "Hoo!" cried he, putting up his hands; "they are just not worth a d—. They can't walk, they can't ride, they can't nurse." "Ah, you have no wife," said I, in a soothing tone. "A wife!" he shouted; "I should kill her." "With kindness?" "Ugh!" he answered, "with a poker. Look at these chits here, dawdling by the fountain. What are they doing now, what have they done all day? Fed and dressed. They have changed their clothes three times, and had their hair washed, combed and curled three times. That is their life. Have they been out for a walk, for a ride? Have they read a book, have they sewn a seam? Not a bit of it. How do your ladies spend their time? They put on good boots, they tuck up their skirts, and hark away through the country lanes. I was in Hampshire once; my host was a duke; his wife was out before breakfast, with clogs on her feet and roses on her cheeks; she rode to the hunt, she walked to the copse; a ditch would not frighten her, a hedge would not turn her back. Why, our women, poor, pale —." "Come," I said, "they are very lovely." "Ugh!" said the saucy fellow, "they have no bone, no fibre, no juice; they have only nerves; but what can you expect? They eat pearl-ash for bread, they drink ice-water for wine; they wear tight stays, thin shoes, and barrel skirts. Such things are not fit to live, and, thank God, in a hundred years not one of their descendants will be left alive."

When looking at these sweet New England girls, as they go trooping past my window, I cannot help feeling that with this delicate pallor, winsome and poetic as it looks to an artist in female beauty, there must be lack of vital power. My saucy friend had got some inkling of the truth. Would that these dainty cousins of ours were a trifle more robust! I could forgive them for a little rose-blush on the cheek; at present you can hardly speak to them without fearing lest they should vanish from before your face.

Woman in her time has been called upon to endure a great deal of definition. In prose and in verse, she has been called an angel, a harpy, a saint, an ogress, a guardian, a fate; she has been likened to a rose and a palm, to the nightshade and the upas; she has been painted as a dove and a gazelle, a magpie and a fox. Poetry has made her a fawn, a nightingale, a swan, while satire has represented her as a jay, a serpent, and a cat. By way of coming to a middle term, a wit described her as, A good idea — spoiled! Wit, poetry, satire, only exhaust their terms; for how can a phrase describe an infinite variety?

A lady, as a single type, would perhaps be easier to define than woman; she would certainly be easier to express by an example. Asked to produce a perfect woman, I might hesitate long, comparing strength and weakness, merit and frailty, so as to get them in the most subtle relations to each other. Asked to produce a perfect lady, I should point to Miss Stars at Washington, Mrs. Bars of Boston, and to many more. Not that perfect ladies are more common than perfect women; they are far less common; but we seize the type more easily, and we know in what soils to expect their growth. A typical woman is a triumph of Nature; a typical lady is an exercise of Art.

Among the higher classes in America, the traditions of English beauty have not declined; the oval face, the delicate lip, the transparent nostril, the pearl-like flesh, the tiny hand, which mark in May Fair the lady of high descent, may be seen in all the best houses of Virginia and Massachusetts. The proudest London belle, the fairest Lancashire witch, would find in Boston and in Richmond rivals in grace and beauty whom she could not feign to despise. Birth is one cause, no doubt, though training and prosperity have come in aid of birth. In some of our older colonies, the people drew their blood from the very heart of England in her most heroic time and mood, when men who were born of gentle mothers flung themselves into the great adventure for establishing New States. The bands who came out under Raleigh's patent, under Brewster's guidance, were made up of soldiers, preachers, courtiers, gentlemen; some coming hither to seek a fortune, others to find an asylum; and though crowds of less noble emigrants followed after them — farmers, craftsmen, menials, moss-troopers, even criminals — the leaven was not wholly lost. The family names remained. Even now, this older race of settlers keeps its force in some degree intact; making the women lovely, the men gallant and enduring, in the fashion of their ancient types. This higher range of female beauty, which is chiefly to be found in the older cities and in families of gentle race, is thoroughly English in its style; reminding the stranger of a gallery of portraits in a country-house; here of Holbein and Lely, there of Gainsborough and Reynolds. Leslie, I think, brought some of his sweetest English faces from the United States.

In many of the younger cities of the Union, there is also a great deal of beauty, backed by a good deal of wit and accomplishment; but the beauty of these younger cities (at least that sample of it which I see here in Saratoga, and that which I saw a little while ago at Lebanon Springs) is less like the art of

Gainsborough and of Reynolds than that of Guido and of Greuse. Much Flemish blood is in it. The skin is fairer, the eye bluer, the expression bolder, than they are in the English type. New York beauty has more dash and colour, Boston beauty more sparkle and delicacy. Some men would prefer the more open and audacious loveliness of New York, with its Rubens-like rosiness and fulness of the flesh; but an English eye will find more charm in the soft and shy expression of the elder type. In New York, the living is more splendid, the dressing more costly, the furnishing more lavish, than in New England; but the effect of this magnificence, as an educating agent, is found to be rather upon the eye than upon the soul. May I illustrate my meaning by example? In Fifth Avenue, New York, you may find a mansion which has cost more money to build than Bridgewater House in London, and in which the wines and viands served to a guest may be as good as any put on an English board; but an American would be the first to feel how wide an interval separated these two houses. One house belongs to wealth, the other to poetry. One boasts of having marble columns and gilded walls, the other of possessing Raphael paintings and Shakespeare quartos. In Fifth Avenue there is a palace, in Cleveland Row there is a shrine.

Some of this difference is what I find (or fancy) between the beauties of Boston and Richmond and those of Washington and New York. Of course, I am not speaking of shoddy queens and petroleum empresses; these ladies make a class apart; who, even when they chance to live in Fifth Avenue, have no other relation to it than that of being there, like the hickories and limes. I speak of the real ladies of New York, women who would be accounted ladies in Hyde Park, when I say that, as a rule, they have a style and bearing, a dash, a frankness, a confidence, not to be seen among their sisters of either New England or Old England. "I was very bad upon him; but I got over it in time, and then let him off," said a young and pretty woman of New York to a friend of mine; speaking of her love affairs, in the secrecy of a friendship which had lasted two long days. By *him*, she meant a swain whom she, in the wisdom of sixteen summers, had chosen from the crowd; one whom, if the whim had only held her a trifle longer, she might have made her husband by lawful rites. The girl was not a brazen minx, such as a man may sometimes see in a train, in a river boat, playing with big words and putting on saucy airs, but a sweet and elegant girl, a lady from brow to instep, with a fine carriage, a low voice, a cultured mind; a piece of feminine grace, such as a man would like to have in a sister and strive to compass in a wife. Her oddity consisted, first, in the thing which she said; next, in her choice of words; in other phrase, it lay in the difference between an English girl's and an American girl's habits of thought with regard to the relations of men and women. "I was bad upon him, but I let him off," expresses, in very plain Saxon words, an idea which would hardly have entered into an English girl's mind, and, even if it had so entered, would never have found that dry and passionless escape from her lips.

In that phrase lay hidden, like a pass-word in a common saying, the cardinal secrets of American life: — the scarcity of women in the matrimonial market: and, the power of choosing and rejecting which that scarcity confers on a young and pretty girl.

## CHAPTER V.

#### Squatter Women.

The fruits of this excess of males over females in the American market are not confined to young damsels who flirt and pout in Saratoga, in Newport, and at the Falls; they come in equal harvests to the peasant girls of Omaha, St. Joseph, and Leavenworth. In the western country, the excess of males is greater than it is in the eastern, with advantages to match on the part of our fairer sex.

Among the many points of difference between life in the Old World and life in the New, none comes more vividly to the eye than the daily contrast between the gait, dress, speech, and occupations of females in the lower ranks. If Fifth Avenue is a paradise for women, so, each in its own degree, is the mill, the ranch, the oil-spring, the rice-field, and the farm-yard.

I am old enough to recall with a smile my boylike indignation when I first saw females labouring in the open country; not with the men, their fathers and sweethearts, as they might do for a day of haymaking in my own Yorkshire; but alone on the hillsides, in gangs and parties, gaunt and wasted things, ill-clad, ill-fed, pallid with toil, and scorched by the sun. This trial happened to me in beautiful Burgundy, on the slopes of sweet Tonnerre, to which I had gone in the heyday of youth, full of dreams and pastorals. Good old Josephine, poor little Fan, how my heart used to ache for you, as you trotted off in the early day, in your old flap hats, your thin calico skirts, and thick wooden clogs, with the rakes and hoes in your hands, the jar of fresh water on your heads, the basket of brown bread and onions on your arms, leaving that lazy old Jean, who called one of you wife, the other of you daughter, asleep in his crib! How my fingers used to twitch and claw the air when, later in the day, the rascal would come out into the street, shake himself into good humour, gabble about the news, play his game of dominoes at the estaminet door, and enjoy his pipe of tobacco on the steps of St. Pierre! Since that boyish day, I have seen the feminine serfs at their field-work in many parts of the earth; the Celt in Counaught, the Iberian in Valentia, the Pawkee in Colorado, the Fellaheen in Egypt, the Valack in the Carpathian mountains, the Walloon in Flanders, the Negress in Kentucky; but I have never yet been able to look down on this grinding and defacing toil without flushing veins. After so much waste, it was rather comical to find Loo Sing making beds and Hop Chang washing clothes.

In my own country, the peasant girl is not everything that poets and artists paint her. In spite of our Mayday games, our harvest-homes, and many other country pastimes, relics of an older and a merrier age, the English peasant girl is a little loutish, not a little dull. As a rule, she is not very tidy in her person, not very neat in her dress, not very quick with her fingers, not very gainly on her feet. The American girl of the same rank in life is in every respect, save one, her superior.

It may come from living in a softer climate, from feeding on a different diet, from inheriting a purer blood; but from whatever cause it springs, there can be no dispute about the fact, that in Lancashire and Devonshire, indeed, in every English shire, you find among the peasant women a degree of personal beauty nowhere to be matched, as a general rule, and on a scale for comparison, in the United States. Many American girls are comely, many more are smart; but among the lower grades of women, there is no such wide and plentiful crop of rustic loveliness as an artist finds in England; the bright eyes, the curly locks, the rosy complexions, everywhere laughing you into pleasant thoughts among our Devonshire lanes and Lancashire streets. But then comes the balance of accounts. With her gifts of nature, our English rustic must close her book, in presence of her keen and natty American sister.

A few weeks ago, I rode out with a friend to see Cyrus Smith, a peasant farmer, living in 'the neighbourhood of Omaha. Omaha is a new city, built on the Missouri; a place that has sprung into life in a dozen years; and is growing up like a city in a fairy tale. Yesterday it had a hundred settlers, to-day it has a thousand, to-morrow it may have ten thousand. Twenty years ago, the Omaha Indians lodged under its willows, and the king of that tribe was buried on horseback, by the adjacent bank. Now, it is a city, with a railway line, a capitol, a court-house, streets, banks, omnibuses, hotels. What Chicago is, Omaha threatens to become.

Cyrus Smith is a small squatter, living near a tiny creek, in a log-hut, on a patch of forest land, which he has wrung from nature by the toil of his hand, the sweat of his brow. The shed is not big, the plot of land is not wide. Within a narrow compass, everything needful in the way of growing stuff and rearing stock, for a family of young children, must be done; cows must be stalled; pigs littered, poultry fed. There is no wealth to spare in Smith's ranch; the fare is hard, the living is only from hand to mouth; yet on the face of affairs, there is no black sign of poverty, of meanness, such as you would see about an Irish hovel, a Breton cabin, a Valack den. Walk up this garden way, through these natty little beds of fruit trees, herbs, and flowers. This path might lead to a gentleman's villa; for the road is wide and swept, and neither sink nor cesspool, as in Europe, offends the eye. Things appear to have fallen into their proper places. The shed, if rough, is strong and snug; a rose, a japonica, a Virginia creeper, climbing round the door. Inside, the house is so scrupulously clean, that you might eat your lunch as comfortably off its bare planks as you could from the shining tiles of a Dutch floor. The shelves are many, the pots and pans are bright. Something like an air of gentle life is about you; as though a family of position, suddenly thrown upon its own resources, had camped out in the prairie, halting for a season on its march. In the little parlour, there is a vase of flowers, a print, a bust of Washington. You see at one glance that there is a bright and wholesome woman in this house.

Annie Smith is the type of a class of women found in America — and in some parts of England — but nowhere else. In station she is little above a peasant; in feeling she is little below a lady. She has a thousand tasks to perform; to light her fires; to wash and dress her children, to scrub her floor, to feed her pigs and fowls, to milk her cows, to fetch in herbs and fruits, to dress and cook the dinners, to scour and polish her pails and pans, to churn her butter and press her cheese, to make and mend the clothes; but she laughs and sings through these daily toils with such a gay humour, such a perfect taste, such an easy compliance, that her work seems like pleasure and her care like pastime. She is neatly dressed; beyond, as an Englishman might think, her station in life, were it not that she wears her clothes with a perfect grace. Her hands feel soft, as though they were cased all day in kid. Her manner is easy, her countenance bright. Her idiom, being that of her class, amuses a stranger by its unconscious sauciness of tone. But her voice is sweet and low, as becomes her sex, when her sex is at its best. Oddities of expression you will hear from her lips, profanities never. Dirt is her enemy; and her sense of decency keeps the whole homestead clean. She rises with the sun, oftentimes before the sun; her beds are spotless, her curtains and hangings like falling snow. A Sicilian crib, with sheets unwashed for a year, is a thing beyond her imagination to conceive. No herding with the kine, no sleeping in the stable, so common in France, in Italy, in Spain, is ever allowed to her son, to her servant, by Annie Smith. A Kentish barn in hop-time, a Caithness bothy in hay-time, would appear in her eyes to be the abomination of abominations. Her chicks, her pigs, her cattle, are all penned up in their roosts, their styes, their sheds. A Munster peasant puts his pig under the bed, a Navarrese muleteer yokes his team in the house, an Epirote herdsman feeds his goats in the ingle, and an Egyptian fellah takes his donkey into his room. But these dirty and indecent habits of the poor people in our lazy Old World, are not only unknown but incomprehensible to American women of the grade of Annie Smith.

Another thing about her takes the eye; the quality of her everyday attire. In England, our female rustics, from the habit of going to church on Sundays, have caught the custom of dressing themselves in better clothes on one day of the week than on the other six days. They have, in fact, their Sunday gowns, compared with which their ordinary wear is nothing but mops and rags. In these respects their sisters in Italy and France resemble them; the contadina having her festa boddice, the paysanne her saint's-day cap. The Suffolk farmer's wife, whom you see coming out of church to-day, her face bright with soap, her bonnet gay with ribbon, has no objection to be seen by you again tomorrow, grimy with dirt, and arrayed in patches. Not so in America; where Annie thinks it would be in bad taste for her to dress gaudily one day, and shabbily six days. True economy, she says, makes her dress herself cleanly and nattily, even when the materials of her gown are poor. One good suit is cheaper than two suits, though one of them may be coarse in texture and mean in make. Good dressing is a habit of the mind, not a question of the purse. Any woman with a needle in her hand may be tidily dressed.

All round Smith's holding near Omaha lies a colony of bachelors; four men out of five in this territory being without wives. Annie feels some influence from the common fact; her house is a pleasant centre for the young; and as bachelors are apt to grow untidy in their ranches, she finds it pleasant fun to suggest without words the blessings which accrue to a man who is lucky enough to procure a wife.

How sad to think that every man who may deserve it cannot win the prize!

## CHAPTER VI.

### Feminine Politics.

If all that I hear from the female politicians of these New England States — particularly from those of beautiful Burlington — be true, the great reform coming forward in the United States is a moral and social change; a reform of thought even more than of society; a change in the relations of man to woman, which is not unlikely to write the story of its progress on every aspect of domestic life.

Compared with such a revolution, all other issues of right and wrong — bases of representation, negro suffrage, reconstruction, State rights, repudiation, and the like — are but the topics of a day, trifles of the vestry, accidents of time and place, in two words, parish politics. Domestic reform, when it comes at all, must be wide in scope, grave in principle. The question now on trial in the United States is said by these female advocates of Equal Rights to be, in effect, neither more nor less than this: Shall our family life be governed in the future of our race by Christian law or by Pagan law?

We have had an old saying among us, that "a clever woman can make any man she pleases propose to marry her;" and this London phrase, I am told, has been very much the New York fact.

In the face of our surplus million of spinsters,

the saying is a pleasantry, as you may see at any crush-room, kettle-drum, and croquet-party. Who does not know a hundred clever women, among the brightest of their sex, who are dropping down the stream, unbidden to the church upon its banks? If that saying about a clever woman being able to marry whom she pleased, were true, should we always hear it with a smile? Who would risk meeting those clever women? "Come now, and bring the lady that owns you," were Lady Morgan's coquetting words to a friend whom she was coaxing to drop in upon one of her morning concerts. Yet the brilliant Irish lady wrote, that in all ages, in all climates, women have behaved like saints, and been treated like serfs. It is not a female saying, that a woman can marry any one she likes.

"Woman and her Master" gave a voice to that cry of the female heart, which has led London into founding a Ladies' College in a side street, a Ladies' Club over a pastry-cook's shop; which has helped New York into calling congresses of maids and matrons on love, marriage, divorce, with the kindred topics of natural selection, artistic maternity, and the mediatorial privilege of the sex.

It must be owned, that as yet our own female politicians have made but puny efforts to free themselves from the bonds of law. With us, Reform has to wait on times and seasons. In English society, the masculine mind still bears the bell, and the most daring of her sex cannot hope, when she lays her hand on our forms and canons, to have the laughter on her side. She knows it will be against her. Not so her American sister; come what may, the Vermont heroine, the New Hampshire reformer, has no dread of being baffled by a sneer. Mary Cragin may renounce her marriage vows, Anna Dickenson may mount the platform, Mary Walker may put on pantalettes. What do they care for men's jests and gibes? Young girls being now in brisk demand, women are free from all fear of misadventure and neglect, even though they should presume to look the great question of their destinies in the face. Prudence of the trading sort having no part in what these ladies may say and do, they are free to think of what is right in fact, of what is sound in law; to come together in public, to teach and preach, to defy the world, and to hold a parliament of their own. Why should they not? If men may meet in public to discuss affairs, why may not women? Are parish politics more important to a people than domestic politics?

No man with eyes and heart will say that everything in relation to our home affairs has yet been placed on a perfect footing — that justice everywhere reigns by the side of love — that behind the closed door, the curtained window, all the relations of husband and wife, of parent and child, are tempered and ennobled by a Christian spirit. If this cannot be said, with even a show of truth, then we have failed as yet to plant on our hearths the religion of love. And if we have failed in our attempt after a Christian life, why may not the reasons of our failure be asked in a public place, in presence of those whom it concerns? But whether men may think it right or wrong to put such queries, American damsels have begun to think, to write, and to vote upon them. Domestic life is said to be woman's sphere; domestic reform, then, is feminine work. Some of these Vermont politicians have got far beyond writing and voting on domestic love. Oneida Creek and Salt Lake City — communities founded by Vermont men — are practical replies to the one great question of our day — What shall be done to reform the abuses of our social and domestic life?

All the ladies who have entered these lists in favour of their sex — who have begun to preach and write on woman's place in the household, on equality of male and female, on free trade in love, on slavery in marriage, on the right of divorce, on sexual resurrection — whether they lift up their voices with a Margaret Fuller at Brook Farm, a Mary Cragin at Oneida Creek, an Antoinette Doolittle at Mount Lebanon, a Belinda Pratt in Salt Lake City, an Eliza Farnham of New York — have gone back, in these debates, to the very first of First Principles: the absence of all guiding light, of all settled law, even of all safe tradition on the subject of domestic life, compelling them, in search of evidence, to question books, to waylay facts, to criticise codes. These ladies have entered on their task with spirit. No sphere has been too high, no abyss has been too deep, for their prying eyes. They have soared to Olympus, they have plunged into Hades, in search of examples of the actual working of a law of love. They have turned to Syria and to Egypt, to Athens and to Rome; they have appealed to nature and to art, to poetry and to science; they have disputed the story of Eve, denied the wisdom of Lycurgus, invaded the seclusion of Sarah's tent. From every country they have sought an argument, a warning, a reproof. They have gone down to the threshing-floor with Ruth, they have read the story of Aspasia, they have dwelt on the fate of Lucretia, they have invoked the spirit of Jane Grey. In every land they have found a model and a moral; and though the model may vary with woman's height, and colour, and education, the moral is said to be everywhere the same. Until the new era — which their newest prophetess, Eliza Farnham, has been good enough to describe as Woman's Era — dawned upon the sex in America, they have found that the female had been treated by the male, sometimes as a toy, often as a victim, generally as a chattel, always as a slave. Where, they ask, in glancing through the story of our race, can a woman's eye find anything to admire? Let her pass into an Arab harem, into a Hindoo zenana, into a Kaffir kraal, into a New York hotel, into a Pawnee wigwam, into a Mayfair house, and what will she find in these female cages? Equality of the sexes, freedom of the affections? Nowhere. East and west, north and south, she will find little more than government by the strong. As regards higher principles of order, she will see alike in the Christian house and in the heathen cave, the same confusion of ideas, the same difference of laws — the greatest confusion, the wildest divergence, being found, it is alleged by some, in the United States.

In no country under heaven, say these female reformers of domestic life, is the woman held equal to the man. An Arab is allowed to marry four wives; a Jew gives daily thanks that he was born a man; a Persian doubts, in spite of the Koran, whether his concubine has any soul. Baron and feme, the lord and his woman, are the rough old English names of husband and wife. In America, in the midst of liberty and light, the station of woman has hardly been improved — if she measures the improvements by Christian lengths. At Onondaga, in New York, the principal people have petitioned the legislature in favour of abolishing all the laws against seduction. Even in Boston, in Philadelphia, in New York, the most refined, the most wealthy societies of America, her position, say these female politicians, is little better than it is among the Perfectionists and Mormons, even when she has given herself to the man of her choice. See what she has to yield! She must give up to him her name; she must cease to be a citizen; she must transfer to him her house and land; she must sink herself in her new lord. What more does the negress yield on being sold as a slave? In legal jargon, the married lady becomes a feme covert; a creature to be treated as an infant, who can hardly do either right or wrong; a change which, while shielding her on one side, robs her on the other of all her natural rights. No court, no canon, no society, does the woman justice. What is a wedding-ring but a badge? What is a harem but a prison? What is a house but a cage? Why should man have the court, the camp, the grove, while woman has only love? Why should not girls aspire to shine in the senate, to minister in the church? Why may not Elizabeth Stanton represent New York in Congress? Why should not Olympia Brown have the charge of souls at Weymouth? Must women be condemned for ever to suckle fools and chronicle small beer? Such ladies as Lucy Stone and Mary Walker put these queries to the world, while an army of wives and maidens waits for its reply.

The very names which the two sexes use towards each other in wedlock imply, it is alleged, the relations of lord and slave. Husband means master; wife means servant. In many parts of America, as in England north of the Trent, a woman of the lower classes never speaks of her husband otherwise than as her "master;" and a husband of the same parts, in the same class, would never talk of his wife except as his "woman;" when he would let you see that he pets her, as his "little woman." Are these relations, ask indignant Eliza Farnham, persuasive Caroline Dall, to be the lasting bases of the married state in a free, a pacific, and a religious land?

No other topic ever did, no other topic ever will, excite in the human breast so keen a curiosity as the relations of man to woman, of woman to man; two bright and plastic beings, unlike in form, in genius, and in office; yet linked by nature in the strongest bonds; fated, as the case may be, to make each other either supremely wretched or supremely blest. Society is the fruit of these relations. Law is but a name for the order in which they exist. Poetry is their audible voice. All epics, tragedies, and stories, rest upon them, as the fountains of our nobler and our finer passions. From these relations spring our highest love and our sternest hate. Minor dramas play themselves out. Simpler problems get themselves solved. To wit: the rules which govern the relations of man with man — whether as prince and subject, priest and laic, father and son, creditor and debtor, master and slave — are found to have been obeying for ages a certain law of growth, which has been softening them, until the old, harsh spirit of pagan law has been all but wholly cast out of our daily life. Is it the same with those rules which govern the more delicate relations of man with woman? In no very large degree.

Is it not a sad, surprising fact, that in the nineteenth century of gospel light, the laws under which women are compelled to live in wedlock should be worse in America than they are in Asia? In Turkey, marriage makes a bond woman free; in the United States (if we believe these champions of Equal Rights) it turns a free woman into a slave. In the East, polygamy is dying out; the only quarter in which it is being revived is the West.

Is it true that our domestic affections lie beyond the sphere of law? Men like John H. Noyes, women like Harriet Holton, say so boldly; and at Wallingford and Oneida Creek, the sexes have deposed all human codes and agreed to live with each other by the light of grace. But this opinion, with the practice which depends upon it, is the fancy of a small, though an active and seducing school. The world thinks otherwise; for the world believes in a law of God, even though it may have ceased to confide in a law of man.

## CHAPTER VII.

#### Husbands and Wives.

About the main facts which lie at the root of this feminine discontent with existing rules, there is hardly any debate among men of sense. All who have eyes to see, admit them. When you enter upon a study of that nameless science, so often in our thoughts, which may be called the Comparative Anatomy of Domestic Life, you are certainly met on the threshold of inquiry by the astounding fact, that the rights of woman in wedlock would seem to have had scarcely any connexion with the scheme of Christian progress. All other rights appear to increase with time. The subject wins concessions from his prince; the layman rises to the level of his priest; the child obtains protection against his sire; the debtor secures some justice from his creditor; the slave is freed from his owner; but hardly any change in her condition, hardly any improvement in her standing, comes to the wedded wife. As a mere chattel, a damsel may be safe; as a wedded wife, the mistress of a home, the law takes hardly any note of her existence; even after all the changes wrought by a dozen years of reform, the law may be described as almost blind to her sufferings, deaf and dumb to her appeals.

When you compare the relations of man with

man, and of man with woman, in Asia and America, you are struck at every turn by unsuspected contrasts. Whether you look on man as a citizen, as a laic, as a son, as a debtor, as a servant, you find him better placed before the law in America than in Asia. Could a fellah in Damascus dare to say in a rich man's presence, "I am as good as you?" Could the ryot of Lucknow answer to his lord, "Go to, my vote is as good as yours, and I will not serve you?" Would not such an offender be despatched to the gateway and punished with twenty stripes? But, is there any such difference between Damascus and Boston, between Lucknow and Philadelphia, in respect of the relation of man with woman? Not at all. The contrast lies another way, for in Turkey, in Persia, in Egypt, in Mohammedan India, the privileges of married women stand on a surer footing as to justice than they do in Massachusetts, Pennsylvania, and New York. If you doubt this fact, take down from your shelves the Hidayah, that legal code which an English lawyer has to administer in our Indian courts, and your doubts will pass away into quaint surprise. On opening the Hidayah, you will find that the harem life, which many of those who have never seen it are content to picture as a drama of poisons, bowstrings, slaves, and eunuchs, is guarded and secured, so far as the females go, by a host of wise and compassionate rules, which are not to be broken with impunity by the stronger sex. Many persons here in Boston imagine that a harem is a jail, an Oriental wife a slave; though a very slight acquaintance with Mohammedan law would show them that an English wife is far worse off as a woman than any of her swarthy sisters of Egypt and Bengal.

In one short chapter of a dozen pages, Blackstone set down in his Commentaries all that he could find in our books about the legal relations of an English husband to the woman whom he makes his wife. In the Hidayah (Arabic Commentaries) the chapters which contain the rules defining the relations of a Moslem husband to his Moslem wife, are long enough to fill a volume. A New England advocate of Equal Rights for the two sexes, would describe our English code — and after it the American code — as making a free woman into a serf by the machinery of a civil contract and a solemn rite; in some respects as worse than into a serf, since, by the mere act of marriage, it cancels all the rights to which she may have been born, takes away her family name, disposes of her goods and lands, and gives her person into the power of a man who may squander her fortune and break her heart. How far would such a description by the New England advocate be unfair? Who does not know that such cases may be occurring in any town? We need not look for examples in the divorce courts: — they meet us in these streets, they cry aloud to us from these balconies. Our common law gives up the wife so thoroughly into her husband's power, that a woman, who comes to the altar young, confiding, beautiful, and rich, may be compelled by brutal treatment, for which the law can give her no redress, to quit it, after a dozen years, an outraged woman with a ruined fortune and a wasted frame. One course, and only one, can save her from the risk of these evils: — a settlement made on her account with the law before she has entered on the fatal rite.

Nothing so gross and cruel towards a young and loving girl could happen in either Turkey, Persia or Mohammedan India. In a Moslem country, every right which a female, whether rich or poor, enjoys by her birth, remains with her, a sacred property, to her death. No man can take it from her. After she has passed from her father's house into her husband's home, she is still a citizen, a proprietor, a human being. She can sue her debtors, and recover her own in the open courts. All the privileges which belong to her as a woman and as a wife are secured to her, not by the courtesies that come and go, but by actual text in the book of law. A Moslem marriage is a civil act, needing no mollah, asking no sacred phrase. Made before a judge, it may also be unmade before a judge. But the Eastern contract is in this respect more logical than the Western contract, that it gives to the man no power upon the woman's person beyond what the law defines, and none whatever upon her lands and goods. A Persian, a Turkish bride, being married to a man of her own rank and creed, retains in the new household which she enters to become the soul, her separate existence as her father's child. A New England bride, on being married to a man of her own rank and creed, becomes lost in him. A Turkish wife is an independent and responsible person, knowing what is right and wrong, and with the same faculty of receiving and devising property which she held in her spinster days. What is hers is not her lord's. She may sue her debtor, without the concurrence of her nearest friend. She may receive a pension, sign a bond, execute a trust. Compared against her Asiatic sister, what a helpless being an American lady seems!

The very first lesson, then, to be drawn from this study of the Comparative Anatomy of Domestic Life, is that rules of law are not beyond some sort of fair and equal application, even in the midst of those secresies which feed, and those sanctities which guard, the love of husband and wife. Such rules of law are found in Asia. They exist in Cairo, in Bagdad, in Delhi, in a hundred cities of the East. Our own magistrates have to take account of them in India; where the most intricate questions of domestic right, — questions relating to dowry, to divorce, to preference, to maintenance, to conjugal fidelity, are brought before the courts, and require to be considered and decided on principles utterly unknown in Westminster Hall. In dealing with such cases between man and woman, we have to lay aside our Statutes at large, our civil law and common law; to forget our jargon of baron and feme, covert and sole. The Suras of Mohammed supply us with the principles, the Commentaries of Abu Yusuf with the details, of a practicable Moslem code. Who, then, in the face of our large Indian experience, will be bold enough to say, that law cannot be made to reach the innermost recesses of a household? In Delhi, in Lucknow, in Madras, not to speak of Cairo, of Damascus, of Jerusalem, law penetrates to the nursery and to the bridal chamber. Of course, there may be secret tyrannies in Asia, as there may be in America; violence of the strong against the weak may be fierce as the passion, subtle as the genius, of an Oriental race; but the excesses of a Moslem husband find no sanction either in the silence or in the provisions of his actual code. If he does wrong, he does it as wrong, and with the fear of punishment in his heart. When a man commits an abuse of the harem, however trifling, he knows that for the victim of his temper there is a swift and sure appeal to an impartial judge.

But how, it may be asked, does a married woman come to have a higher security against oppression in an Asiatic city than in American cities? Surely it cannot be because those Asiatic cities are Moslem in creed while these American cities are Christian? Nothing in our Gospel makes a Christian wife a slave; and in its sweet tenderness to woman, the Gospel stands high above the Koran, high above every other book. Why, then, is the law of Christendom so harsh to wedded women, while that of Islam appears to be so mild?

This question goes deep down into the roots of things, and a full answer to it would supply the motto for that revolution which the female politicians declare to be coming upon American social life.

## CHAPTER VIII.

#### Domestic Law.

When the New England seeker after better things than she can find just now in a woman's lot, turns aside, with her aching heart, from the wrongs of time towards the promise of a golden age of justice, in she knows not what new cities of Bethlehem, Wallingford, Lebanon, Salt Lake, the sites of her new experiments in living, no man will say that she is troubled without cause. Let her remedy be sought in the right place or in the wrong, the evil is dark and vast; pervading the whole community, and passing in its degrees of shame, from the delicate tortures of the boudoir down to the rough brutalities of the street. Even here in Boston, with all its learning, all its refinement, all its piety, the wrongs of women are so gross that Caroline Dall confessed to a female audience she could neither lay them bare nor speak of them by their proper names. Yet on all these sufferings of the weaker sex, the American law is silent, the American magistrate is powerless. How, ask the reformers, have these evils grown upon us?

That prior question of how it has come to pass that a Turkish, Persian, Egyptian lady enjoys in marriage a securer state than her paler sister of Boston, Richmond, New Orleans, would open up for us a glimpse of some forgotten truths; since it would start a second question — How have we Christians come by our marriage laws, and how have the Mohammedan nations come by theirs? The answer is not far away; for the facts are written broadly in our histories, minutely in our statutes. We get our marriage laws from the Pandects; the Moslems get theirs from the Koran. In this difference of origin, lies the secret of their difference in tone and spirit. Our laws have a civil and commercial source; theirs have a moral and religious source.

Here, indeed, an inquirer strikes his axe upon the root. Our life is a divided duty; a moral life based on the Gospel, a family life based on the civil law. While our morals have their root in Christianity, our statutes have their root in Paganism. And thus it is, in the main degree at least, that woman's griefs in marriage, and in all the relations of sex and sex, have come upon her, like many other evils in our social body, from the fact that we derive our morals from one source, the Gospels, our laws from another source, the Pandects.

One of the sorry jests in which we are apt to array our falsehoods, says that our English and American codes of law are founded on the precepts of our faith. Let us try this dogma by a test. A just and pious man, fresh from his study of Holy Writ, shall walk with the Bible in his hand, into the Supreme Court of the United States, and shall then and there try to persuade the presiding judge that the Sermon on the Mount is good American law, binding on every follower of Christ. Have you any kind of doubt as to what would become of that just and pious man? You know that the judge would pity, the advocate quiz, the audience mock, and the officer seize him. Remove the scene from the Capitol at Washington, to the gateway of Damascus. In the Oriental city, such a man might go before the cadi, Koran in hand, assured that his citations from the holy book would be heard; and if his views of them were sound, that they would govern the verdict to be given. And the reason is plain. An Oriental has not two laws; one for the street, another for the gate; one for his harem, a second for his mosque. His moral life and his civil life have one source, one end, and he finds no war between the teachings of his cadi and his priest. In Boston, in New York, we have a moral code which only on two or three points of moment approaches the edge of our domestic code. What do our judges know of Christ, of Moses, and of Abraham? As lawyers, nothing. These names are not among those which may be quoted in our acts and commentaries. The judges who dispense our law have heard of Justinian, of the civilians; but of the immutable precepts of our faith, the divine foundations of our moral life, they are powerless, as magistrates on the bench, to take any public and judicial note. They must abide by the text; a mixture of the Saxon common law and of the Roman civil law.

A prime result of our laws being Pagan while our morals are Christian, is the fact, so strange and bewildering to an Oriental, that, with us, the practice of virtue is regarded as a private affair, a thing between a man and his Maker only, not, as with the

Moslems, between a man and his fellow. Thus, in Boston, in New York, no law compels a man to be chaste, compassionate, dutiful. One of those wits who speak truth in jests and parables, has said that, in our society, a rich, unscrupulous sinner may contrive to break every commandment in the decalogue, without losing his place either at good men's feasts or in ladies' cabinets. If he is great in evasion, pleasant in manner, choice in hospitality, he may run the whole round of offence, from following false gods to coveting his neighbour's wife. His only art is to avoid being seen by the police. Is that parable untrue? What man who drives in Fifth Avenue, who walks on yon Common, shuts his eyes on the world so far as to dream that our manners are all alike? You need not be a cynic to see that fashion sits down to its meat and wine, day after day, year after year, with wretches who, in any part of Islam, would be taken before the cadi and beaten on the feet. With two exceptions, perhaps, a sinner may break the ten commandments openly, in these public streets, and no one shall lay hands upon him. While he refrains from killing his foe and robbing his friend, he is safe. What magistrate on the bench would think of asking whether a man accused before him bowed to a false god, put away graven images from his house, abstained from the use of oaths, kept holy the Sabbath day, honoured his father and mother, respected the purity of his neighbour's wife, drove out the sin of covetousness from his soul? Not one. And why?

Because the magistrate in his office on the bench

is the minister, not of our moral system, but of our civil code.

The truth is, we English and Americans have hardly yet embraced Christianity as a scheme of life. We find our religion at church, and when we have sung our psalms, and breathed our prayers, we go back into the streets to be governed for another week by our pagan law. Our courts of justice have no authority to notice moral offences, unless they happen to have been injurious to a fellow-citizen in either his peace or his purse. Mere lack of honour, virtue, reverence, goes on our bench for nothing. A wretch may curse his parents, may profane the Sabbath, may worship stocks and stones, without earning for himself the penalty of a stripe. The same wretch may break his wife's heart, may squander his child's estate, may destroy his friend's happiness, yet he shall escape all punishment of his crimes. Some of the darkest transgressions in the sight of God, — the God whose will we obey, — are treated by the code under which we live as of no more moment than the whimsies of a child. Fornication is not condemned. Seduction is treated as a wrong done, not to the girl, who may be its victim, but only to the owner of her service. Adultery is classed with such small injuries as theft; a loss of property rather than of purity and credit; and the man whose name may have been tarnished for ever by a seducer, must plead against the destroyer of his peace, not his outraged honour, but the loss of his daughter's service, of his wife's society. In some of the United States, they have gone a little way towards rounding off these lines of separation between Christian morals and the civil code. In New York, a fellow may be lodged in gaol for seducing girls; but the legislatures have hardly, as yet, even touched the fringe of a mighty evil. Those Onandago reformers of the law who petitioned in favour of replacing the felon's cell by a bridal wreath, — going back to the Mosaic plan of considering the act of seduction as an act of marriage — have no remedy to suggest for the still darker outrage of seducing and debauching a married woman. Nor can they find one under a law which treats the crimes of seduction and adultery as a wrong to the man's estate, but not to his moral life.

In all the advancing schools of American thought, this topic is discussed, the evil is admitted, a remedy is sought. At Oneida Creek they have put an end to adultery by abolishing marriage. At Mount Lebanon they have done the same thing by prohibiting love. At Salt Lake, again, they have checked the evil by punishing adultery with death. But these sectional trials leave the law intact, and the courts and legislatures of the Union are continually being vexed by petitions in favour of substituting some higher rule for the one in vogue. Will they ever find such a rule while they cling to the code of Justinian in preference to the word of God?

In a Moslem country, the Prophet's word is law, each line a command, each sura an institute. The Prophet's object being, according to his lights, to promote among his people not only the public peace, but holy living, his precepts were adapted to the regulation of every act of a believer in the harem, in the mosque, in the bazaar. On the other side, our Saviour's word has only obtained in our western society the force of a moral precept, which every one may adopt, and every one may reject, at pleasure.

Again, our pagan statutes seem to have been framed for service only in the public streets. We have a saying that our house is our castle; it is so sometimes, in a wide and wicked sense. No writ runs in it. Law pauses at the threshold; and the crown itself, the majesty of public right, can only break those portals after due solemnities and in the wake of some atrocious crime. In a Moslem harem, no such feudal secresy is found. Every room in a house is open to the Koran; every act of the lord must be conformable to rule; and a man's wife, his child, his slave, may cite the Koran against him. In Islam, every one knows the law by heart; the Koran being a text which can never fall out of date. All Moslem jurists must adopt this text, which they are only free to expound within certain limits, and every cadi may go back to the original in his day of doubt. The basis of public justice is the same in every age and in every land. In states like England and America, we have no great body of divine, indisputable law, by which all queries might be answered, all problems might be solved. When a case arises in our courts, which no enactment appears to meet, where do our judges look for guidance? Do they turn to the Gospels? Do they read St. Paul? They never think of such a course. The Gospels make no part of our legal store. If we teach the decalogue in our infant-schools, and preach it in our chapels, we make no use of it in our law courts. Proud, as it would seem, of our Pagan code, which puts so much of our conduct into contrast with our creed, we make a boast of this freedom from restraint, and only on our grand occasions, as it were, admit the presence in our midst of a purer law.

Now it is one of the open facts of our modern societies in London and New York, that a woman's rank in the family is either high or low according to the loyalty with which we follow that Gospel law of love which the courts of justice may, if they please, ignore. A Turk is not permitted by the cadi to set aside *his* Sermon on the Mount as a precept for Sundays, for good women, for men in childhood and old age. Even in the privacy of his harem, an Asiatic is governed by some kind of moral and religious rules; while an American is governed in his home only by legal and commercial precepts, from which every moral and religious feeling may have been utterly divorced. Thus it happens that an Oriental wife, though she may be living in the state of polygamy, has in some capital points a wider freedom in her circle than the most highly cultured lady of New York.

Is that the end of our long endeavour after a Christian life? No religious man or woman thinks so; and at this moment a thousand busy brains and gentle hearts are working on the problem of our passage from this stage of growth into a religion of higher truth. Some of these seekers after better things may be groping in the dark; looking for light where light is not; but in so far as they are seeking honestly and with earnest heed to get into the better way, they deserve our study and respect.

Foremost among these seekers after light, are the Brethren of Mount Lebanon in the State of New York.

## CHAPTER IX.

###### Mount Lebanon.

On a sunny hill-side, three miles south of New Lebanon Springs, (a watering-place in the upper country of the lovely river Hudson, at which idlers from New York and Massachusetts spend the hot weeks of summer, lounging in frame sheds, flirting under chestnuts, driving over broken roads, sipping water from the well — which a negro has just told me that a horse may drink without doing itself any harm!) stands a group of buildings, prim and yet picturesque; the chief home of a religious body, small in number, singular in dress and in ideas, and only to be found, as yet, in the United States.

This village is Mount Lebanon, the chief home and centre of a celibate people, founded by Ann Lee; known to scoffers as a comic institution unattached, under the name of the Shaker Village; Shaker being a term of mockery and reproach, like most of our religious names; one which the members meekly accept, and of which they are shyly proud. Among the elect they are known as the United Society of Believers in Christ's Second Appearing.

Needing a little rose-water, I asked a friend where the best might be got. "You must apply," he said, "at any of the stores where they sell

Shaker scents." Inquiring about the best place for collecting American shrubs and flowers, my companion said, "You must ride over to Mount Lebanon, as no one in either New York or Massachusetts can match the Shakers in producing seeds and plants." My curiosity was piqued. Why should the villagers of Mount Lebanon excel the rest of their countrymen in such an art? Of course, I knew that the Essenes were florists and seedsmen, as well as rearers of bees and growers of herbs and corn: but then those Hebrew anchorites lived in a time when husbandry was contemned as a servile art, unfit to occupy the thoughts, to engage the hands, of free men; and they gave themselves up to a life of field labour, not for the profits which it might bring them, but as an exercise of the spirit and a trial of the flesh. In the neighbourhood of Mount Lebanon — a ridge of wooded hills, furrowed with bright dales and glades, and with tiny becks of water running east and south from the Springs — no man affects to despise farming as a lowly craft, the work of women and of slaves; on the contrary, all the best talents of this region are invested in the land; and renown of its kind lies in waiting for the man who shall produce from his acres the finest and most ample crops. "Why, then," I asked my friend, "where all are striving to excel in the art of producing plenty from the soil, should the Shakers of Mount Lebanon be the only seedsmen in the state?" "Guess," said he, after a moment's thought, "it is because they give their minds to it."

This saying about the Shakers giving their minds

to the culture of land may be used as a key to unlock nearly all the secrets of Mount Lebanon. As you climb up this green hill-side from the pretty hamlet of New Lebanon, you may see in the clean roads, in the bright swards, in the trim hedges, more than all else, in the fresh meek faces of men and girls, and in the strange sad light of their loving eyes, how much has been done in a few short years towards converting this corner of New York State from a rugged forest, the haunt of Iroquois and Lenni Lenape, into the likeness of an earthly Eden. The rough old nature shows itself near. Yon crests and tops are clothed in their primæval woods, though the oaks and chestnuts are now in their second growth. Rocks crop out, and stones lie about you. Much of the land has never been reclaimed. The paths are all open; and every man with a gun may shoot down game, as freely as he might in the prairies of Nebraska. But the hand of man has been laid on the soil with a tight, though a tender grasp; doing its work of beauty, and calling forth beauty in exchange for love and care. Where can you find an orchard like this young plantation on our left? Where, save in England, do you see such a sward? The trees are greener, the roses pinker, the cottages neater, than on any other slope. New Lebanon has almost the face of an English valley, rich with the culture of a thousand years. You see that the men who till these fields, who tend these gardens, who bind these sheaves, who train these vines, who plant these apple-trees, have been drawn into putting their love into the daily task; and you hear with no surprise that these toilers, ploughing and planting in their quaint garb, consider their labour on the soil as a part of their ritual, looking upon the earth as a stained and degraded sphere, which they have been called to redeem from corruption and restore to God.

The plan, the life, the thought of Mount Lebanon are written in its grassy streets. This large stone building on your right — an edifice of stone in a region of sheds and booths — is the granary; a very fine barn, the largest (I am told) in America; a cowshed, a hay-loft, a store-house, of singular size and happy contrivance; and its presence here, on a high place, in the gateway, so to speak, of the community, is a typical fact.

The Granary is to a Shaker what the Temple was to a Jew.

Beyond the barn, in the green lane, stands North House, the dwelling of Elder Frederick and Elderess Antoinette (in the world they would be called Frederick W. Evans, and Mary Antoinette Doolittle), co-heads of this large family in the Shaker Society. Below their house, among the shrubs and gardens, lies the Visitors' house, in which it has been my fortune to spend, with Frederick and Antoinette, a few summer days. Around these buildings rise the sheds and stores of the family. Next come a host of gardens, in which the Baltimore vine runs joyously up poles and along espaliers; then the church, lying a little way back from the road, a regular white frame of wood, plain as a plank, with a boiler roof, a spacious, airy edifice, in which the public service of the society is sung and danced on Sunday, to the wondering delight, often the indecent laughter of a crowd of idlers from the Springs. Near by stands Church House, of which Elder Daniel and Elderess Polly (in the world, Daniel Crossman and Polly Reed) are the co-heads; with the school, the store, at which pretty trumperies are sold to the Gentile belles. Beyond these buildings, higher up the hill, stands South House, East House, and some other houses. In all these dwellings live families of Shakers. Elder Frederick is the public preacher; but every family has its own male, its own female head. One family lives at Canaan, seven miles distant, to which I have made a separate visit; while just beyond the crest of yon hill, in the State of Massachusetts, you find another society — the settlement of Hancock.

No Dutch town has a neater aspect, no Moravian hamlet a softer hush. The streets are quiet; for here you have no grog-shop, no beer-house, no lock-up, no pound; of the dozen edifices rising about you — work-rooms, barns, tabernacle, stables, kitchens, schools, and dormitories — not one is either foul or noisy; and every building, whatever may be its use, has something of the air of a chapel. The paint is all fresh; the planks are all bright; the windows are all clean. A white sheen is on everything; a happy quiet reigns around. Even in what is seen of the eye and heard of the ear, Mount Lebanon strikes you as a place where it is always Sunday. The walls appear as though they had been built only yesterday; a perfume, as from many unguents, floats down the lane; and the curtains and window-blinds are of spotless white. Everything in the hamlet looks and smells like household things which have been long laid up in lavender and rose-leaves.

The people are like their village. These dreamers are soft in speech, demure in bearing, gentle in face; a people seeming to be at peace, not only with themselves, but with nature and with heaven. Though the men are oddly attired — in a sort of Arab sack, with a linen collar, and no tie, an under vest buttoned to the throat and falling below the thighs, loose trousers rather short, and broad-brimmed hat, nearly always made of straw — they are grave in aspect, easy in manner, with no more sense of looking comic in the eyes of strangers than either an English judge on the bench or an Arab sheikh at his prayer. The women are habited in a small muslin cap, a white kerchief wrapped round the chest and shoulders, a sack or skirt dropping in a straight line from the waist to she ankle, white socks and shoes; but apart from a costume neither rich in colour nor comely in make, the sisters have an air of sweetness and repose which falls upon the spirit like music shaken out from our village bells. After spending a few days among them, seeing them at their meals and at their prayers, in their private amusements and in their household work, after making the personal acquaintance of a score of men, of a dozen women, I find myself thinking that if any chance were to throw me down, and I were sick in spirit, broken in health, there would be few female faces, next after those of my own wife and kin, that would be pleasanter to see about my bed. Life appears to move on Mount Lebanon in an easy kind of rhythm. Order, temperance, frugality, worship — these are the Shaker things which strike upon your senses first; the peace and innocence of Eden, when contrasted with the wrack and riot of New York. Every one seems busy, every one tranquil. No jerk, no strain, no menace, is observed, for nothing is done, nothing can be done, in a Shaker settlement by force. Every one here is free. Those who have come into union came unsought; those who would go out may retire unchecked. No soldiers, no police, no judges, live here; and among the members of a society in which every man stakes his all, appeal to the courts of law is a thing unknown. Unlike the Syrian Lebanon, she has no Druse, no Maronite, no Ansayri, no Turk, within her frontier; peace reigns in her councils, in her tabernacles, in her fields. Look at these cheery urchins, in their broad straw hats and with their dropping sash, as they leap and gambol on the turf, laughing, pulling at each other, filling this green hill-road with the melodies only to be heard when happy children are at play. Their hearts are evidently light. Look at these little blue-eyed girls (those two with the curly heads are children of a bad mother, who eloped last year with a neighbour, when their father was away in the field with Grant), very shy, and sweet, and clean, and comely are they in their new attire; if ever you saw little girls like angels, surely these are such.

Yet, is it not strange to us that young men and young women should be found living in this beautiful place, in the midst of peace and plenty, without thoughts of love? And is it not sad to reflect that those merry boys and girls, whose voices come in peals of laughter down the lane, will never, if they stay in this community, have little ones of their own to play on the village sward?

The Shaker is a monk, the Shakeress a nun. They have nothing to say to this world; yet their church, so often described as a moral craze, a religious comedy, a ritual of high jinks, at best a church of St. Vitus, not of St. Paul, will be seen, when we come to understand it, to have some singular attractions. The magnetic power which it is exercising on American thought would, of itself, compel us, even though we should be found unwilling hearers, to sit out the comedy and try to comprehend the plot.

## CHAPTER X.

#### A Shaker House.

During the days which I have been spending at North House, the guest of Frederick and Antoinette, I have had every opportunity given to me of seeing and judging for myself the virtues and failings of the Shaker brethren. I have been eating their food, lodging in their chambers, driving in their carriages, talking with their elders, strolling over their orchards; I have been with them of a morning in the field, at noon by the table, at night in their meeting-rooms; watching them at their work, at their play, at their prayers; in short, living their life, and trying to comprehend the spirit which inspires it.

My room is painfully bright and clean. No Haarlem vrouw ever scraped her floor into such perfect neatness as my floor; nor could the wood of which it is made be matched in purity except in the heart of an uncut forest pine. A bed stands in the corner, with sheets and pillows of spotless white. A table on which lie an English Bible, some few Shaker tracts, an inkstand, a paper knife; four cane chairs, arranged in angles; a piece of carpet by the bed-side; a spittoon in one corner: complete the furniture. A closet on one side of the room contains a second bed, a washstand, a jug of water, towels; and the whole apartment is light and airy, even for a frame house. The Shakers, who have no doctors among them, and smile at our Gentile ailments — head-aches, fevers, colds, and whatnot — take a close and scientific care of their ventilation. Every building on Mount Lebanon — farm, granary, mill, and dwelling — is provided with shafts, fans, flappers, drafts, and vents. The stair-way is built as a funnel, the vane as an exhauster. Stoves of a special pattern warm the rooms in winter, with an adjustment delicate enough to keep the temperature for weeks within one degree of warmth. Fresh air is the Shaker medicine. "We have only had one case of fever in thirty-six years," says Antoinette: "and we are very much ashamed of ourselves for having had it; it was wholly our fault."

North House, the dwelling of Elder Frederick's family, has the same whiteness and brightness, the same order, the same articles in every room. Antoinette led me over it yesterday, from the fruit cellars to the roof, showing me the kitchens, the ladies' chambers, the laundries, the meeting-rooms, and the stoves. My friend William Haywood (civil engineer to the City of London) and his wife were with me; the engineer was no less smitten by surprise at the singular beauty and perfect success which the Shakers have attained in the art of ventilation, than the lady was charmed by the sweetness, purity, and brightness of the corridors and rooms. Males and females dwell apart as to their rooms, though they eat at a common table, and lodge under a common roof. "How do you treat a man who comes into union with his wife and children —

that sometimes happens?" Antoinette smiled, "Oh, yes! that happens pretty often; they fall into the order of brother and sister — and make very pretty Shakers." "But," said the lady, "they see each other?" "That is so," answered Antoinette; "they live in the same family; they become brother and sister. They do not cease to be man and woman; in forsaking each other, they only cease to be husband and wife." Some of these ladies who live under Frederick's roof in North House, have husbands (as the world would call them) living close beside their rooms; but they would hold it to be a weakness, perhaps a sin, to feel any personal happiness in each other's company. They live for God alone. The love that is in their hearts — so far as it is capable of bearing mundane fruit — ought to be shed on each of the saints alike, without preference on account of either quality or sex.

Is it always so? After this morning's early meal, Antoinette, who had come into my room, where Frederick and some of the Elders had already dropt in for a social chat, in answer to some of my wondering worldly questions, told me, in the presence of four or five men, that she felt towards Frederick, her co-ruler of the house, a special and peculiar love, not as towards the man, and in the Gentile way, as she had heard of the world's doings in such matters, but as towards the child of grace and agent of the heavenly Father. She told me, also, that she had sweet and tender passages of love with many who were gone away out of sight — the beings whom we should call the dead — and that these passages of the spirit were of the same kind as those which she enjoyed with Frederick. The functions which these two persons exercise in the family, as male and female chiefs, give them the privilege of this close relation, — this wedlock of the soul, if I may use that phrase to express a sympathy which, not being of the world, has no worldly words to represent it.

The ladies usually sleep in pairs, two in a room; the men have separate rooms. One bed is made to slide beneath another, so that when the chamber is arranged for the day-time, there is ample space and a sense of air. Nothing in these apartments hints that the people who occupy them seek after an ascetic life. All the ladies have looking-glasses in their rooms, though they are sometimes told, in love, to guard their hearts against the abuse to which these vanities might lead. "Females," says Frederick in his homely humour, "need to be steadied, some." The dress of these ladies, though the rule is strict as to shape, is not confined to either a single material or a single colour. On some of the pegs hang dresses of blue cotton, lawn stuff, white muslin; and even at church a good many of the ladies appear in lilac gowns, a colour which becomes them well. "We leave the individual taste rather free," says Frederick; "we find out by trial what is best; and when we have found a good thing, either in a dress or in anything else, we stick to it."

These Shakers dine in silence. Brothers and sisters sit in a common room, at tables ranged in a line, a few feet apart. They eat at six in the morning, at noon, at six in the evening; following in this respect a rule which is all but uniform in America, especially in the western parts of this continent, from the Mississippi river to the Pacific Ocean. They rally to the sound of a bell; file into the eating-room in a single line, women going up to one end of the room, men to the other; when they drop on their knees, for a short and silent prayer; sit down, and eat, helping each other to the food. Not a word is spoken, unless a brother should need some help from a brother, a sister from a sister. A whisper serves. No one gossips with her neighbour; for every one is busy with her own affairs. Even the help that any one may need is given and taken without thanks; such forms of courtesy and politeness not being considered necessary in a family of saints. Elder Frederick sits at the end, not at the head, of one table. Elderess Antoinette at the other end. The food, though it is very good of its kind, and very well cooked, is simple; being wholly, or almost wholly, produce of the earth; tomatoes, roast apples, peaches, potatoes, squash, hominy, boiled corn, and the like. The grapes are excellent, reminding me of those of Bethlehem; and the eggs — hard eggs, boiled eggs, scrambled eggs — are delicious. The drink is water, milk, and tea. Then we have pies, tarts, candies, dried fruits and syrups. For my own part, being a Gentile and a sinner, I have been indulged in cutlets, chickens, and home-made wine. "Good food and sweet air," says Frederick, "are our only medicines." The rosy flesh of his people, a tint but rarely seen in the United States, appears to answer very well for his assertion, that in such a place no other physic is required. These people say, they want no Cherokee medicines, no plantation bitters, no Bourbon cock-tails, none of the thousand tonics by which the dyspeptic children of New York whip up their flagging appetites, and cleanse their impure blood. Frederick has a fierce antipathy to doctors. "Is it not strange," says he, "that you wise people of the world keep a set of men, who lie in wait for you until by some mistake of habit you fall sick, and who then come in, and poison you with drugs?" How can I reply to him, except by a little laugh?

No words being spoken during meals, about twenty minutes serves them amply for repast. One minute more, and the table is swept bare of dishes; the plates, the knives and forks, the napkins, the glass, are cleaned and polished, every article is returned to its proper place, and the sweet, soft sense of order is restored.

A man has little inducement to dally with the cherry wine; and as no cigar has ever been allowed to profane the precincts of North House, I rise after a cup of black coffee, and, joining a knot of Brethren, stroll into the fields.

Dropping with Frederick into the schools, the barns, the workshops, I have learned that the Shaker estate on and around Mount Lebanon consists of nearly ten thousand acres of the best woodland and lowland in the state of New York. For a long time, as lots fell into the market, the family has been buying land; but they have now got as much as they can cultivate; more, indeed, than they can cultivate by their own forces; and for some years past they have been compelled, by the extent of their family estates, to hire labourers from among the world's people in the villages about. As they are never angry, never peevish, never unjust (I have heard this said elsewhere, by men who hate their principles and traduce their worship), Gentile labourers come to them very freely, and remain as long as they are allowed to stay. These smiths in the forge by the roadway are World's People; that lad in the cart is a cottager's son; those fellows making hay in the meadow are Gentiles working on the Shaker lands. These labourers have come to Mount Lebanon to live and learn. They get a very fine schooling, and are paid for being at school. No other farming in America reaches the perfection that is here attained; and a clever young lad can hardly pass a season among these fields and farms without picking up good habits and useful hints.

But the chiefs of Mount Lebanon can see that this system of mixed labour, this throwing of the saint and sinner into a common society, for the sake of gain, is foreign to the genius of their order. Such a system, if it were to grow upon them, would be hostile to their first conception of celestial industry; it would, in fact, by the operation of a natural law, degenerate into a feudal and commercial business, in which the Saints would be bankers and proprietors, the sinners would be labourers and serfs. That is not an end for which they have denied themselves so much. Even their wish to do good among the Gentiles must not lead them into what is wrong;

and they are now considering whether it may not be wiser for them to part with all their surplus lands.

I need not say that any estate which has been for a few years under Shaker ploughs and spades will sell in the market at what would otherwise be considered as a fancy price.

Climbing up the hill-road from the pretty valley of New Lebanon, I notice the fine rows of apple-trees growing in the hedges, after the English fashion in some counties. Elder Frederick, himself of English birth, is pleased to hear me speak of the old country. "Aye," says he, "this green lane, and these fruit-trees, carry me back to my old home." Americans of the higher class, when they are grave and tender, always speak of England by the name of Home. The trees in this lane are planted with care and skill; but I notice, not without curiosity, that in the midst of so much order, one apple-tree stands a little from the line. "How do you prevent the passers-by — the lane being a public highway — from snatching at the fruit and injuring your trees?" The Elder smiles; if the flush of light in his soft blue eyes can be called a smile. "Look at yon tree," says he, "a little in front of the rest; that is our sentinel; it bears a large, sweet apple, which ripens a fortnight before the others; and it is easy for every one to reach. Those who want an apple pluck one from its boughs, and leave the other trees untouched." Is it always true, that the children of this world are wiser in their generation than the children of light?

Every man among the Brethren has a trade;

some of them have two, even three or four trades. No one may be an idler, not even under the pretence of study, thought, and contemplation. Every one must take his part in the family business; it may be farming, building, gardening, smith-work, painting; every one must follow his occupation, however high his rank and calling in the church. Frederick is a gardener and an architect. We have been out this afternoon seeing an orchard of apple-trees which he has planted, the great barn which he has built, and I have good grounds for concluding that this orchard, this barn, are the finest works of their kind in the United States. The Shakers believe in variety of labour, for variety of occupation is a source of pleasure, and pleasure is the portion meted out by an indulgent Father to his Saints.

The ladies at Mount Lebanon — all these sisters are ladies in speech, in manner, in garb — have no out-door work to perform; some are employed in the kitchen, some in waiting on others (duties which they take in turn, a month for each course), some in weaving cloth, some in preserving fruit, some in distilling essences, some in making fans and knick-knacks. Maple-syrup is an article for which they have a good demand; they make rose-water, cherry-water, peach-water; they sew, they sing, they teach children, and teach them very well. Their school is said to be one of the best for a good general education in New York State.

## CHAPTER XI.

#### Shaker Union.

VERY little study of the work achieved by the followers of Ann Lee will serve to show that Shakerism as an actual fact in the domestic life of America (whatever we may think about its origin), is far from being a mere folly, to be seen on a Sunday morning with a party of ladies, a diversion between the early dinner and the afternoon drive, to be wondered at, laughed over, and then forgotten as a thing of no serious consequence to the world. Mount Lebanon is the centre of a system which has a distinct genius, a strong organization, a perfect life of its own, through which it would appear to be helping to shape and guide, in no slight and unseen measure, the spiritual career of the United States.

In many of their ideas the Shakers would appear to be followers of the Essenes, and in the higher regions of emotion they seem to be wielding the same sort of power as that Hebrew society of beemasters and seedsmen.

Their church is based on these grand ideas: — The kingdom of heaven has come; Christ has actually appeared on earth; the personal rule of God has been restored. In the wake of these ideas, dependent upon them, follow many more: — the old law is abolished; the command to multiply has ceased; Adam's sin has been atoned; the intercourse of heaven and earth has been restored; the curse is taken away from labour; the earth, and all that is on it, will be redeemed; angels and spirits have become, as of old, the familiars and ministers of men.

Only the elect, it is said, are aware of these mighty changes having taken place on the earth; for the many are blind and deaf, as they were of old, knowing not the Lord when He calls them into union. A few are chosen by the grace of God, and in the hearts of His own elected ones He reigns and works. On being called by Him, men die to the world, forgetting in their new and heavenly stage of existence its rivalries, its pleasures, and its passions. In the firm belief of these people, the call which they obey is not to a mere change of life, but to a new life of the soul, in which the world has no share. Birth and marriage are at an end; death itself has become to them only a change of dress, a shedding of the visible robe of flesh for an invisible glory of the spirit.

These fundamental ideas control the Shaker policy, inward and outward.

Thus, no man can be born into their body, as no member of their church can marry. In union, as they say it is in heaven, the sexes must dwell apart; love must be celibate, in spirit and in fact, shedding its worldly and unregenerate relations with the flesh. Most of those who come into union at Mount Lebanon are young men and girls, such as in Italy and Spain would go into monasteries and convents; but when married people enter, they must agree in future to live apart, in chastity and obedience, pure from all fancies and desires of their olden life. Again; no man may be drawn by lures of the world into union with their body, since the elected ones are strictly forbidden to make use of any lure, any argument, with the Gentile. God, it is said, in His own time, in His own way, will draw to Himself the men whom He has made His own. The Shaker union being considered by them as the heavenly kingdom, they are to have no part in the task of peopling it with Saints; for the children of grace can be called into His rest by none but God. Heaven must be sought of man; she will never again go forth to seek; her day of missionary work being past.

If the community of Saints gives much to a member, it demands much from him as the price of his fellowship. When a man is led upwards of the spirit into a yearning after peace, he must offer at the gates of Mount Lebanon everything which a man of the world would prize; his wealth, his case, his glory, his affections; for what is earth to heaven, and what is man in the sight of God? Before an applicant can be received into this society, he must throw his possessions into a common fund; he must consent to labour with his hands for the general good; he must forget all ranks and titles of the world; he must abandon his house and kin, his books and friends; he must tear himself away from his wife and child. On these high terms, and on no other, can a Gentile enter into the Shakers' rest.

Yet thousands of persons enter into union. Mount Lebanon is but one of eighteen Shaker societies, which are scattered throughout these United States. Besides New Lebanon, there are two other settlements in New York State: namely, Water Vliet, in Albany county (the original Shaker society), and Groveland in Livingston county. There are four villages in Massachusetts: Hancock (the birth-place of Lucy Wright) and Tyringham in Berkshire county, Harvard and Shirley in Middlesex county, two in New Hampshire: Enfield in Grafton county, Canterbury in Merrimac county; two in Maine: Alfred in York county, New Gloucester in Cumberland county; one village in Connecticut: Enfield in Hartford county (the birth-place of Meacham, the Shaker Moses); four villages in Ohio: White Water in Hamilton county, Water Vliet in Montgomery county, Union village in Warren county, and North Union in Cuyahoga county; two in Kentucky: Pleasant Hill in Mercer county, and South Union in Logan county. In spite of their hard life, — what may seem to us their very hard life, — the Shakers increase in number; the census of 1860 reporting them as more than six thousand strong.

Of course, when they are measured against the thirty millions of Christian people living in the United States, some six or seven thousand celibate Shakers may appear of but small account; and this would be the truth, if the strength of spiritual and moral forces could be told in figures, like that of a herd of cattle and a kiln of bricks. But if numbers are much, they are far from being all. One man with ideas may be worth a Parliament, an army,— nay, a whole nation, without them. The Shakers may not be scholars and men of genius. In appearance they are often very simple; but they are men with ideas, men capable of sacrifice. Unlike the mass of mankind, who live to make money, the Shakers soar above the level of all common vices and temptations, and from the height of their unselfish virtue, offer to the worn and wearied spirit a gift of peace and a place of rest.

No one can look into the heart of American society without seeing that these Shaker unions have a power upon men beyond that of mere numbers. If a poll-tax were decreed, they might pay less into the exchequer than the Seceders, the Second Adventists, the Schwenkfelders, and the Jews; but their influence on the course of American thought is out of all comparison with that of such minor sects. The Shakers have a genius, a faith, an organisation; which are not only strange, but seductive; which have been tried in the fire of persecution, and which are hostile to society as it stands. A Shaker village is not only a new church, but a new nation. These people, who have just been out with me in the fields and lanes, know nothing of New York, of the United States. They are not Americans; and have no part in the politics and quarrels so often raging around them. They vote for no President; they hold no meetings; they want nothing from the White House. The right to think, vote, speak, and travel, is to them but an idle dream; they live with angels, and are more familiar (as they tell me) with the dead than with the living. Sister Mary, who was sitting in my room not an hour ago, close to my hand, and leaning on this Bible, which then lay open at the Canticles, told me that the room was full of spirits; of beings as palpable, as audible to her, as my own figure and my own voice. The dreamy look, the wandering eye, the rapt expression, would have alarmed me for her state of health; only that I know with what sweet decorum she conducts her life, and with what subtle fingers she makes damson tarts. Frederick has the same beliefs; if you like the word better, the same illusions. What need can such a people have for votings and palavers? God is their only right; obedience to His will their only freedom.

That such a community should be able to exist in the United States, is a sign; that it should have seized upon men's affections, that it should have become popular and prosperous, growing without effort, conquering without conflict, drawing towards itself many pure, unselfish persons from the adjoining towns and states, is little less than a judgment on our churches. And such, in truth, the Shakers call it.

On entering into union with the believers, then, a convert must withdraw himself from the world; paying off all debts, discharging all bonds and trusts, renouncing all contracts, cancelling all wills and settlements, giving up all friends and kinsmen, as though he were parted from them by the grave. Indeed, the call which he receives from God is to be accepted as a proof that his past life as a sinful creature is at an end:—in final words, the flesh is deposed and the world put away.

On being received into the union, he no longer regards the earth as a spoil to be won, but as a pledge to be redeemed. By man it fell, by man it may be restored. Every one chosen of the Father has the privilege of aiding in this redemption; not only by the toil of his hands, by the contrivance of his brain, but by the sympathy of his soul; covering the world with verdure, filling the air with perfume, storing the granary with fruit.

The spirit in which he puts his hand out is a new one to him. Hitherto, the earth has been his servant; now it is his partner, bound to him by celestial ties. He looks at the face of nature with a lover's eyes, and the great passions of his heart, directed from his money, from his wife, now turn upon the garden and the field. But he understands that labour alone is not enough; he knows that the labourer must be worthy of his task, that this fanaticism must be guided by angelic wisdom. According to Shaker theories, the earth has been accursed and darkened by human passions, and must be redeemed into beauty by human love. Man makes the landscape smile and frown; the plant you train will grow into your likeness; and if you would have a lovely garden, you should live a lovely life. Such at least is the Shakers' thought.

My Gentile brother, if we were to flout this notion as a crazy dream, the fact would still remain, and we should have to account for it as we might, that these Shakers get more out of the earth by love, than we get by our craft. This fact is not a thing to be disputed and denied; the evidence is found in a hundred Broadway stores and London shops. If we deny that the earth will answer love by love, we are bound to explain the beauty and fertility of Mount Lebanon in some other way.

This morning I have spent an hour with Frederick in the new orchard, listening to the story of how he planted it, as to a tale by some Arabian poet. "A tree has its wants and wishes," said the Elder; "and a man should study them as a teacher watches a child, to see what he can do. If you love the plant, and take heed of what it likes, you will be well repaid by it. I don't know if a tree ever comes to know you; I think it may; but I am sure it feels when you care for it and tend it; as a child does, as a woman does. Now, when we planted this orchard, we first got the very best cuttings in our reach; we then built a house for every plant to live in, that is to say, we dug a deep hole for each; we drained it well; we laid down tiles and rubble, and then filled in a bed of suitable manure and mould; we put the plant into its nest gently, and pressed up the earth about it, and protected the infant tree by this metal fence." "You take a world of pains," I said. "Ah, Brother Hepworth," he rejoined, "thee sees we love our garden."

Thus, when a Shaker is put upon the soil, to beautify it by his tilth, the difference between his husbandry and that of a Gentile farmer, who is thinking solely of his profits, is likely to be great. While the Gentile is watching for his returns, the

Shaker is intent upon his service. One tries for large profits, the other strives for good work. Is it strange that a celibate man, who puts his soul into the soil — who gives to it all the affection which he would otherwise have lavished on wife and child — should excel a mere trading rival in the production of fruits and flowers?

## CHAPTER XII.

### Mother Ann.

SITTING with Elder Frederick, who has been taking much pains to make me understand his intricate and difficult code of morals, I have heard how these seedsmen and florists of Mount Lebanon have been made what they are in skill, in gentleness, in temperance — in all the virtues which they display — through loyal obedience to the lessons taught them by Ann Lee; a female saint, who is only known to her followers by the august and holy name of Mother. She may be spoken of as Mother Ann.

As a distinct and sacred people, the Shakers have this peculiar boast among American churches — that, while they are wholly of the New World in thought, in feeling, and in platform, having no life beyond these great waters, they draw the original germ of their existence from the old paternal soil. If they are called to an American paradise, the messenger of heaven who called them into rest was a female English seer.

About a hundred years ago, a poor woman, living at Bolton-on-the-Moors, a bleak and grimy town, in the most stony part of South Lancashire, announced that she had received a call from heaven to go about the streets of her native town and testify for the truth. Her name was Jane; her husband, James

Wardlaw, a tailor, with gifts of speech, had become her first convert and expositor. These poor people had previously belonged to the Society of Friends, in which they had been forward in bearing testimony against oaths, against war, against formality in worship. Living in a hard and rocky district, in the midst of a coarse and brutal population, Jane had seen about her, from her youth upwards, a careless church, a Papist gentry, a drunken and fanatical crowd. Going out into the market-place, she had declared to these people, that the end of all things was at hand, that Christ was about to reign, that His second appearance would be in a woman's form, as had been long ago prefigured in the Psalms. Jane had never said that she herself was the female Christ; but she had acted as though she believed that all the powers of earth and heaven had been given into her hands; receiving converts in His name, confessing and remitting sins, holding communication with unseen spirits. It was assumed by her own people that she was filled with the Holy Ghost; and whatsoever thing she affirmed, in the power of her attendant spirits, had been received by her followers as the Voice of God. But her reign had not been long.

Among the early converts of this female witness had been a girl named Ann Lee, daughter of a poor blacksmith; a girl of parts, though she had never been taught to read and write. Born in Toad Lane (now Todd Street), Manchester, a lane of ale-houses and smithies, Ann had been brought up, first in a cotton-mill, next in a public kitchen; a wild creature from her birth, a prey to hysteria and convulsions; violent in her conduct, ambitious of notice, and devoured by the lust of power. Like many girls of her class, she had been married while she was yet a child; married to a neighbouring lad, a smith of the name of Stanley; a man poorer even than herself. To this man she had borne four infants, all of whom had died in their tender years: and these losses of the young mother may have touched her mind with a morbid repugnance to the offices and duties attending on a woman's share in our common conjugal life. Joining the sect of Jane Wardlaw, Ann also had begun to sally forth into the streets and witness for the truth; lecturing the blacksmiths of Toad Lane, the weavers of New Cross, on the things to come, until the prosy old parish constable had seized her as a nuisance, and the magistrate had sent her to gaol as a disturber of the public peace. While she was lying in prison — Old Bailey prison, on the Irwell — she said a light had shone upon her, and the Lord Jesus had stood before her in the cell, and become one with her in form and spirit. Jane Wardlaw had never yet pretended to have wrestled with so high a power; and when Ann Lee came out of prison, the little church of six or seven persons to whom she told her story, had raised her to the rank of Mother, in place of their foundress, the tailor's wife.

A feminine church had been now openly proclaimed in Manchester and Bolton, with Mother Ann as that queen who was described by David, as that Bride of the Lamb who was seen in the Apocalypse by John. Christ, it was now proclaimed, had come again; not in His pomp and power, as the world expected Him, but in the flesh of a factory girl who could neither read nor write.

As the rough lads and lasses of her native town had only laughed at this pretence of a female church, Ann had received a second revelation from heaven, commanding her to shake the dust of Toad Lane from her feet, to gather up the sheep of her tiny fold, and to seek for them, and for herself, a home in the Promised Land. The spirits who waited upon her, angels and ministers, had drawn her thoughts to America, as the hope of free men and the seat of God's future church. Five males (William Lee, James Whittaker, John Hocknell, Richard Hocknell, James Shepherd) and two females (Mary Partington and Nancy Lee) had been minded to cast in their lot with her; and although the master of the ship in which they sailed from Liverpool had threatened, on the voyage out, to pitch them all into the sea for what he called their indecent conduct, Ann, with her husband Stanley, and her seven disciples, had landed safely in the bay of New York.

The only one of this little band who had felt no true faith in Mother Ann was her husband; but in spite of his want of grace, she had proceeded, on their reaching the Promised Land, to put her gospel of abstinence into force; insisting on the need for living a holy life, and separating herself, a Bride of the Lamb, from her husband's side. Her fixed idea had been, that she and her people should make eternal war against the flesh. By lust man fell from heaven; by abstinence from carnal thoughts he might hope to regain his celestial rank. No form of earthly love could be tolerated in the Redeemer's kingdom. Men called into grace must live as the angels live; amongst whom there is neither marrying nor giving in marriage. Every member, therefore, of her church had been compelled to renounce his yearning after love; the wives consenting to dwell in a house apart from their husbands, the husbands in a house apart from their wives. They had put to themselves this question: If all men, born into the world, are born into sin, and made the heirs of death in the world to come, how can the Saint, when raised from his fallen nature, dare to augment this empire of sin and death?

It would have been hard for Stanley to answer that question from Mother Ann's point of view, otherwise than as she answered it; but her husband, though he could not give his reasons, had felt that, as a married man, he was being badly used. He was no mystic; and when his wife had put her self-denying ordinance into force against him, he had taken up (I am grieved to write it) with another woman of New York. Mother Ann had left him, and had left New York City, going up the Hudson river as far as Albany, then a small frontier town, facing the great wilderness towards the west. Even there her people had found the world too much with them. Pushing out into the backwoods, to a spot then known to the red skins as Niskenna, they had built log shanties, and taken up their abode in the green waste, founding the township now so famous as Water Vliet, the original Shaker settlement in New York.

For three years and six months these strangers had waited in their lonely huts, clearing the forest, tilling the soil, rearing bees and fowls, and waiting for a sign from heaven. They had made no efforts to convert the Gentiles. They had fled from, rather than sought, the society of men. They had preached no sermons, printed no books, written no letters, announced no gospel. Desolation could hardly have been more complete than they found on the Hudson river at Niskenna. But this nest of seven believers in Mother Ann's divine commission, being comforted by angels of the night, had waited and watched for the promised coming-in of the Saints. At length their faith in her promises had been crowned by wonders. A religious revival which had broken out in Albany, spread into the villages of Hancock and New Lebanon, where it had caught up, in its electrical vortices, many substantial sinners, including, among other well-to-do people, Joseph Meacham and Lucy Wright. Joseph and Lucy, with some of their neighbours who had heard of the coming of Ann Lee, had gone over the hills to Niskenna, as a deputation from the revivalist camp (spring of 1780), and after seeing her way of life, hearing her words of peace, and being told of the appearance to her in the Manchester gaol, they had embraced her creed, admitted her right, and become her first disciples on the American soil. Meacham had been adopted by Ann as her eldest son; and the Mother had then declared that, after her time, the power would be given unto him from God to put the kingdom of heaven into perfect order. The result of this visit of Lucy and Joseph to Mother Ann had been the foundation of the Shaker societies in Hancock and Mount Lebanon.

Ann had now fallen into trouble, the inheritance of seers and prophets from of old. The War of Independence being at that time brisk, and the people ardent in the cause, the farmers and woodmen of New York had taken up the notion that these Shakers, who raised their voices against war as the devil's work, had come into the land as enemies, perhaps as spies; a charge which the gentry of Albany told Ann and her disciples they must rebut by taking the colonial oaths. But how were they to take the colonial oaths, seeing that their principles forbade them to swear at all? First, Meacham and the men, afterwards Ann and the women, had been thrown into gaol, where they had been visited by many people, and become a topic of discourse throughout New York. Instead of calming men's minds and putting Ann down, the gentry of Albany soon found that they had been the means of spreading the fame of this strange prophetess through their colony, into both the English and American camps. What could they do with a prisoner who told them she was the female Christ? They had thought her crazy, and they had fancied, she being an English-born woman, that it would be well to send her with a pass into the British lines. With that end in view, she had been sent down the river, but the plan could not be carried into effect on account of the war; and, in the meantime, she had been lodged for security in Poughkeepsie gaol, where she held a little court of her own among her attendant spirits, and left behind her in that town, when she quitted it, memories and influences which have taken shapes in the Spiritualist theories of a later time.

Set free by Governor Clinton (December, 1780), Ann had come out of prison a famous woman; and after three months had been spent by her at Water Vliet, in the midst of her male and female elders, she had started on a tour of exhibition, visiting Harvard in Massachusetts, and many other places in the New England colonies, increasing the number of her disciples, and providing the materials for her future model societies. Her work had been long and toilsome; not without profit to her in many ways; but after twenty-eight months had been spent in these travels, she had returned to Water Vliet, near the Hudson River, in September 1783, wasted in vigour, though she seemed to have become sublimed in spirit. One winter and one summer more she had held on to her task, but in the fall of 1784, she had gathered her disciples round her, given them a promise and a blessing, and after yielding up the visible keys of her kingdom to Joseph and Lucy, as her successors in the male and female headships of the kingdom of God, she had passed away from their sight.

According to the doctrines now held by the Shaker church, Mother Ann did not die, as mortal men and women die; she became changed to the world, transfigured and transformed, made invisible to the flesh through excess of light. From what I have heard and read, it seems to me probable that some of Ann's people were amazed at her disappearance, — an event on which they had not counted; nor could they reconcile it with her story of that second advent in the Manchester gaol, where their Lord had taken flesh in a woman's form. Their faith appears to have been sorely tried; but Joseph Meacham and Lucy Wright — the divinely appointed king and queen of the new kingdom — had proved themselves equal to the moment. With the corpse of Ann before them, they had stoutly affirmed that she was not dead. The Queen foretold by David could never die; the Bride whom John had seen in his vision could never sink into the grave. The Queen had been covered with robes of light; the Bride had passed into the secret chamber. Ann had withdrawn herself for a little while from the world, which had no part in her; but she would live and reign for ever amongst her own true children of the resurrection. The dust before them was nothing but a worn-out garment which the Mother had cast away.

Joseph and Lucy had caused this dust to be lifted up, and put away in a field, not in any sacred place, in any consecrated ground, where it might rest in peace for the final rising; but in a common field, where it might soon be lost and forgotten, where in time the plough would go through it, causing it to mingle with the earth from which it had been drawn. A Shaker expects no further rising of the dead. In his conviction, the dead are now risen, and are even now rising. To be called into grace, is the same as being raised from the dead into a new life. Frederick and Antoinette believe that they have passed through the shadow, that they will die no more, that when their season comes they will only be withdrawn, like Mother Ann, from the world. They are living now, they are firmly convinced, in the Resurrection Order.

## CHAPTER XIII.

#### Resurrection Order.

WHEN Joseph Meacham and Lucy Wright had put the dust of Mother Ann away, telling her people that she had only changed her raiment, being clothed in her celestial robes as Bride of the Lamb, all difficulties appear to have been conquered, and the faith of the wavering to have been made strong. The doctrine was seductive and bewitching. Ann was still living in their midst; in dreams, in ecstasies, they could see her, they could hear her voice. The change which had come upon her, would one day come upon them. How glorious for the saints to think that Death is but a change in the costume of life; that the dissolving soul dies only to the flesh; that the glory to which the elect attain conceals them from the world; but leaves them visible to eyes, audible to ears, which have been purified and exalted by the gift of grace!

To this dogma of the existence of a world of spirits — unseen by us, visible to them — the disciples of Mother Ann most strictly hold. In this respect, they agree with the Spiritualists; indeed, they pride themselves on having foretold the advent of this spiritual disturbance in the American mind. Frederick tells me (from his angels), that the reign of this Spiritualistic frenzy is only in its opening phase; it will sweep through Europe, through the world, as it is sweeping now through America; it is a real phenomenon, based on facts, and representing an actual, though an unseen force. Some of its professors, he admits, are cheats and rogues; but that is in the nature of spirit-movements, seeing that you have evil angels as well as good angels. Man is not the only deceiver. If men are false, is there not one who is the father of lies? When the higher and nether world shall have come yet nearer to the earth — in the riper days of the Resurrection — both good and evil spirits may be expected to have greater power on earth.

Antoinette, who has just been sitting in my room, asserts that she talks with spirits, more freely and confidingly than she does with me; yet I cannot see that Antoinette is crazy on any other point, and she certainly makes neat and sensible speeches. This room, in which I am writing — the guest-chamber of North House — which seems to me empty and still, is to her full of seraphim and cherubim, who keep on singing and haranguing the livelong day. Mother Ann is here present; Lucy and Joseph are present; all the brethren who have passed out of human sight are present — to her. You have only to watch Antoinette for a moment, when you are not yourself engaging her attention, to see, by her hushed face, by her rapt eye, by her wandering manner, that she believes herself in another presence, more revered, more august, than anything of earth. Yes; those whom we Gentiles call the dead are with her; and by this ethereal process of belief, the brethren of Mount Lebanon have conquered death and put an end to the grave.

This morning, when Antoinette first came into my room, I thought she was very grave and sweet; in her hand she held a paper, as though she had brought it in to show me; and on my inquiring what it was about, she laid it on my table, saying it was a song which she had heard in the night, sung by angelic choirs. My eyes ran towards it; and from her way of speaking I could see that she meant to give it me as a parting token. "Sign it, Sister Antoinette," I said, "and let me have it." She wrote her name on the margin of this song; from a perusal of which the reader will see that either the copyist mistook some of the seraphic words, or else that the angels are not particular as to syntax and rhyme.

> Let us ascend the heavenly scale,
>   In purity be rising;
> In deeds of charity and love
>   Let not our souls be wanting.
>
> On the immortal hills of truth
>   Are flowers eternal blooming;
> I long to breathe that fragrant air,
> To join my voice with angels there,
>   So sweetly they are singing.

I do not understand Antoinette to say that this hymn was made by the seraphs expressly for me. She is too simple to indulge in jests; and I could not hurt her mind by any lay remark. Perhaps it may be as well to add that all the chants and marches used by the Shakers in their services are learnt in dreams and reveries. None of their sacred poetry is very good, according to our secular canons, though some of it has a lilt, a fire, that would make effective verse if it had only been managed with a little more art. I have rarely heard a finer effect, of its kind, in music than that produced in the frame church on Mount Lebanon by four or five hundred Shakers, men and women, marching to this chant:

> To the bright Elysian fields,
>   In the Spirit-land I go!
> Leaving all inferior joys,
>   All pleasures below.
>
> For my spirit reaches upward,
>   To that celestial land,
> Where, by the power of truth and love,
>   The Saints as victors stand.
>
> The murmuring of the waters,
>   From the troubled sea of time,
> Can never reach the peaceful shores
>   Of that pure, that happy clime,
> Where angels the banners of love gently wave,
> And where Saints do triumph over death and the grave!

If we may judge by the rules established in this lower world, your angels make much better tunes than rhymes. The Shakers' marches are often very fine.

To Joseph Meacham, Mother Ann's first adopted son on the American soil, and to Lucy, her daughter and successor in the female sphere, the government of this Church descended by divine appointment; and their rule, which is beyond appeal, was made more easy to them by the promise of their departed founder. "The time will come," Mother Ann had said, "when the Church will be gathered into order; but not until after my decease. Joseph Meacham is my first-born son in America; he will gather the Church into order; but I shall not live to see it." And with this promise on her lips she had passed out of mortal sight.

As yet, the believers in Mother Ann being the second incarnation of Christ had been scattered through the world, living in it bodily for the greater part, though they were not of it in the spirit. Joseph and Lucy had drawn these believers apart into settlements: to Water Vliet and Mount Lebanon in New York, to Harvard and Shirley in Massachusetts, to Enfield in Connecticut, to Canterbury in New Hampshire, to Union Village and White Water in Ohio, to Pleasant Hill and South Union in Kentucky. Under their rule, a covenant had been written down and accepted by the brethren. The divine government had been confirmed: elders and deacons, female as well as male, had been appointed; celibacy had been confirmed as binding on the Saints, and community of goods had been introduced among them. When Joseph had also passed out of sight in 1796, he had bequeathed an undivided power to Lucy, who then became the leader, representing Mother Ann, and for five-and-twenty years governing these Shaker societies with the powers of a female Pope. When her time had also come, she named her successor; for who, unless the chosen, shall have the right to choose? But she had named an Elderess, not a Mother; and since her day the title of Mother has been abandoned, no female saint having sprung up among them worthy to bear so august a name. The present female leader of the Society is Betsy Bates; she is simply called Elderess Betsy; she represents the Mother only in the body, for Ann is thought to be herself present among her children in the spirit. The chief elder and successor to Joseph is Daniel Boler, who may be regarded as the Shaker bishop; but the active power of the Society (as I fancy) lies with Elder Frederick, the official preacher and expositor of Shaker doctrine. If the Shaker communities should undergo any change in our day, through the coming in of other lights, I fancy that the change will have to be brought about through him. Frederick is a man of ideas, and men of ideas are dangerous persons in a Society which affects to have adopted its final form. Boler represents the divine principle, Frederick the art and government of the world.

The family at North House contains two orders of members (1) Probationers, (2) Covenanters. The first are men and women who have come in for a time to see how they like it, and whether it likes them. Men in this early stage of the celestial trial retain their private fortunes, and maintain some slight relation to the Gentile world. Men of the second stage may be said, in effect, to have taken the vow of chastity, and to have cast in their lot for good and evil with the brethren. The chiefs have very little trouble, Frederick tells me, with the novices, for any one may go out when he pleases, taking all that he brought in away with him. A poor fellow who puts in nothing, is generally sent away, if he desires to leave, with a hundred dollars in his purse. The rich men give less trouble than the poor, being generally persons of higher culture and of more earnest spirit. One of my female friends in the community, Sister Jane, came in as a child with her father, Abel Knight, one of the first citizens of Philadelphia. She is young, pretty, educated, rich; but she has given up the world and its delights; and if ever I saw a happy-looking damsel, it is Sister Jane.

As regards their notions of the duty of living a celibate life, there is (as Elder Frederick tells me) a great mistake abroad. They do not hold that a celibate life is right in every place and in every society, at all times; they know, that if the rule of absolute self-denial were commonly adopted, the world would be unpeopled in a hundred years; but they say that marriage is a state of temptation to many (as wine-drinking is a state of temptation to many), and they consider that for a male and female priesthood, such as they hold themselves to be as respects the world, this temptation is to be put away. That claim of being a sort of priesthood of the Saints, appointed to serve God and to redeem the world from sin, runs through the whole of their institutions. To this end, indeed, they have passed through death and the resurrection into a state of grace. To this end they have adopted the rule of absolute submission of their own will to the will of God. "We admit," says Frederick, "two orders in the world — one of Generation, one of Resurrection." They claim to stand in the Resurrection order; to them, therefore, the love which leads men into marriage is not allowed. We Gentiles stand in the Generation order, therefore the love which ends in marriage is still for a time allowed. "Generation," says Frederick, "is a great foe to Regeneration, and we give up what is called our manhood as a sacrifice for the world."

"You mean to say, then, that in fact you are offering yourselves as an atonement?" He paused a moment; his blue eyes closed, and when he opened them again, slowly, as if waking from a trance, he smiled.

"The Order of Resurrection," he added, "is celibate, spiritual; in it there is no marriage; only love and peace."

In their social economy, as in their moral sentiment, these Shakers follow the ancient Essenes. They drink no wine, they eat no pork. They live upon the land, and shun the society of towns. They cultivate the virtues of sobriety, prudence, meekness. They take no oaths, they deprecate law, they avoid contention, they repudiate war. They affect to hold communion with the dead. They believe in angels and in spirits, not as a theological dogma, but as a practical human fact.

One circumstance which gives to the Shaker society an importance in the Union far beyond its rivals (Tunkers, Moravians, Mennonites, Schwenkfelders), is the fact of its being much devoted to the work of education. Every Shaker settlement is a school; a centre from which ideas are circulated right and left, into every corner of the land. Men who would laugh at the pretensions of Mother Ann, if they stood alone, can hardly help being touched, if not seduced, in spirit, by avowals like these now following: —

The church of the future is an American Church.

The old law is abolished, the new dispensation begun.

Intercourse between heaven and earth is restored.

God is king and governor.

The sin of Adam is atoned, and man made free of all errors except his own.

Every human being will be saved.

The earth is heaven, now soiled and stained, but ready to be brightened by love and labour into its primæval state.

These propositions, which display the genius of Shakerism so far as it pretends to be a social and political power, at war with the principles and practices of a republican government, are apt to fascinate many men who would object to a celibate life, to a female priest, to a community of goods. With more or less of clearness in avowal, these principles will be found in the creed of every new American church.

## CHAPTER XIV.

#### Spiritual Cycles.

AND how, we ask, so soon as we have left the witcheries of Mount Lebanon behind us, and begun to look on the matter with a purely secular eye, are these eighteen settlements of Shakers recruited? In Rome, in Seville, convents may be fed from the lay society in which the laws of increase hold their natural sway; but in Enfield, at Mount Lebanon, in Groveland, no lay community of Shakers stands outside the church, from which the losses by death can be repaired. The whole church being celibate, the losses by death are fixed and final; so many to the year; the whole generation in thirty years. Calls, fresh calls, must be made under pain of extinction; but how are men to be called from a busy world, from a prosperous society, into a life of labour, chastity, confinement, and obedience? In Italy and Spain, it is found an uneasy task to persuade young men to renounce the affections, even for an indolent service. Nature is strong, and a life without love appears to many of us worse than a tomb. One great branch of the Christian Church, the Latin, has adopted celibacy in principle, making it the rule for its clergy of all ranks, and fostering the practice in its lay societies; but her success in this particular branch of her policy has hardly equalled her efforts;

and in no country of Europe, even in Sicily and Andalusia, has she found willing recruits, except when she has taken them from the world at an early age, and excercised upon them her most potent spells. The Greek, the Armenian, the Lutheran, the Anglican churches, have ceased to fight against nature, though they are all inclined, perhaps, to assign some merit to a virgin life, and to desire a celibate condition for a section of their priests. In all these churches there is something like a balance of advantages in what is given and what is withheld. The position of a priest is one of high respect in the sight of men. The service to which he is called is noble and popular; one conferring rank and power, the right to stand among the highest, to be exempted from labour, to be protected from violence, to be free of great houses, and to find a welcome at good men's feasts. The Shaker has none of these dignities, none of these pleasures to expect in return for his pledge of chastity; in their stead, he has before him hard work, coarse fare, and an ugly dress.

Under a missionary like Khaled, we can imagine converts being made to the Shaker Church; a man who offered you a choice of either Shakerism or death, might be expected to bring proselytes to the fold; but then, these believers have no Khaleds among them; they employ no sword, they exercise no fascination of the tongue and pen. Where, then, do they find recruits? Is the keen New Englander anxious to give up his will, his freedom, and his intellect, in exchange for a fixed belief, a daily drill, and a peasant's toil? Is the rich New Yorker bent on stripping himself of his costly mansion, his splendid equipage, in favour of a coarse habit, a rood of land, and a narrow cell? Is the smart Kentuckyan ready to forswear his rank, his office, his ambition, for a life of daily labour, abstinence, and care?

"No," said Elder Frederick, in one of my parting conversations, "not in ordinary times. In God's own time he must and will; being then divinely touched and rapt, and acting in the spirit of a wisdom higher than the world. It is chiefly in our spiritual cycles that the elect are called."

When the seasons come and go at their usual pace, when the air is still and the minds of men are tranquil, the rich New Yorker, the smart Kentuckyan, would no more dream of coming into union, than of going to live in a Pawnee wigwam or a negro shed. But in the day of spiritual wrath, when the vials are being opened on the land, when sinners run staggering up and down, when the colleges are mute, and the churches of the world stricken dumb, then heaven itself comes forward into line, and, working through her unseen forces, draws to herself the rich, the daring, and the worldly spirit, as easily as a little child. In the hands of God, we are only as the potter's clay. The strong will bends, the proud heart breaks, in His frown. It has been in the midst of these moral and spiritual commotions, that all the new creeds, all the new societies, of America have either risen or gathered strength; not the poor Tunkers, the aggressive Mormons, the celibate Shakers only; but the powerful Methodists, the prosperous Baptists, the rigid Presbyterians, the

## SPIRITUAL CYCLES.   117

fervent Universalists. The Episcopal Church, and the Roman Church may stand aloof; the educated and refining intellect of these elder branches of the Christian society holding that the teachings of Christ and His chosen apostles were final, that the age of miracle is past, and that the gospels are complete. The members of these great conservative churches may ask no day of an especial grace; they may doubt the origin, the efforts, and the fruits of these periodical awakenings of the spirit. They may choose to walk in the old paths, to avoid novelties and eccentricities, to keep their flocks from excitements and illusions. But their younger rivals for dominion, acting, as they say, in the apostolic missionary spirit, have been prompt to seize upon all occasions of drawing souls into the Church. All the new sects and societies of America have wrought, and not without success, in this great field of conversion; the Shakers in a spirit less eager and more confident than the rest. Other sects regard a revival as a movement in the mind inviting them to labour for the good of souls; the Shakers look upon it as a Spiritual Cycle — the end of an epoch — the birth of a new society. Only in the fervour of a revival, says Elder Frederick, can the elect be drawn to God: — that is to say, in Gentile phrase, drawn into a Shaker settlement. Mount Lebanon sprang from a revival; Enfield sprang from a revival; in fact, the Shakers declare that every large revival, being the accomplishment of a Spiritual Cycle, must end in the foundation of a fresh Shaker union.

Thus, it would appear that this wild and weird

phenomenon in the religious kingdom, which some of our Gentile clergy deem an accident, an illusion, answering to no law of life, is to the Shakers the effect of a special providence. Angels are employed upon the work. In the Shaker economy a revival has, therefore, a place, a function, and a power. It is their time of vintage; when the shoots which they have not planted bring them grapes, when the presses which they have not filled yield them oil. They reckon on these periodical revivals as the husbandman reckons on the spring and fall; waiting for the increase which their spiritual cycles bring them, just as the farmers expect their hay-time and their harvest-home.

When the last Ulster revival broke out, I happened to be in Derry; and, having watched the course of that spiritual hurricane from Derry to Belfast, I am able to say that, excepting the scenery and the manners, a revival in Ulster is very much the same thing as a spiritual cycle in Ohio and Indiana.

In this country, the religious passion breaks out, like a fever, in the hottest places and in the wildest parts; commonly on the frontiers of civilised states; always in a sect of extreme opinions, generally among the Ranters, the Tunkers, the Seventh-day Baptists, the Come-outers, and the Methodists.

Methodism, the large religion of America, if we may count the church by heads, was itself the offspring of a kind of revival. John Wesley had tried America, and failed; Whitfield had followed him, and succeeded; the time being more propitious to his work. The early preachers had won their way, as the revivalist preachers still carry on the fight; lodging roughly and faring coarsely; tramping up muddy ridges, sleeping on leaves and deer-skins, tenting among wolves and beavers; suffering from the red-men, from the mean whites, from the besotted negroes, forcing their way into gaols, gin-shops, and hells; searching out poverty, misery, and crime. The revivalist is a fanatic, if you like the word; he speaks from his hot blood, not from his cool head; his talk is a spasm, his eloquence a shriek; but while philosophers may smile and magistrates may frown at his ravings, the swarthy miner, the lusty backwoodsman, the sturdy farmer and carter, confess to the power of his discourse. He does the rough work of the spirit which no other man could do. Trench would be tame, Stanley inaudible, in the prairie; Wilberforce would faint, and Noel would die, of a year on the forest skirt.

Yet a camp-meeting, such as I have twice seen in the wilds of Ohio and Indiana, is a subject full of interest; not without touches, in its humour and its earnestness, to unlock the fountains of our smiles and tears. The hour may be five in the afternoon of a windless October day; when myriads of yellow flowers and red mosses light up the sward, when the leaves of the oak and the plane are deepening into brown, when the maples gleam with crimson, and the hickory drips with gold. Among the roots and boles of ancient trees, amidst buzzing insects and whirring birds, rise a multitude of booths and tents, with an aspect strange, yet homely; for while this camp of religious zealots is utterly unlike the lodgements of an Arab tribe, of an Indian nation, of any true pastoral people on the earth, it has features which recall to your eye and ear the laughters and sounds of an English fair and an Irish wake. Epsom on a Derby Day is not so unlike a revival camp in the woods as many may think. Carts and waggons are unhorsed; the animals tethered to the ground, or straying in search of grass. In a dozen large booths men are eating, drinking, smoking, praying. Some fellows are playing games; some lolling on the turf; others are lighting fires; many are cooking food. Those lads are cutting pines, these girls are getting water from the stream. In the centre of the camp, a pale revivalist marabout, standing on the stump of a tree, is screeching, and roaring to a wild, hot throng of listeners, most of them farmers and farmers' wives, from the settlements far and near; a sprinkling of negroes, in their dirty finery of shawl and petticoat; a few red men in their paint and feathers:— all equally a-blaze with the orator himself, fierce partners in his zeal and feeders of his fire. His periods are broken by shouts and sobs; his gestures are answered by yells and groans. Without let, without pause, in his discourse, he goes tearing on, belching forth a hurricane of words and screams; while the men sit around him, white and still, writhing and livid, their lips all pressed, their hands all knotted, with the panic and despair of sin; and the women rush wildly about the camp, tossing up their arms, groaning out their confessions, casting themselves downward on the earth, swooning into sudden hysterics, straining at the eyes and foaming at the mouth; the staid Indian looking with contempt on these miseries of the white man's squaw, and the negroes breaking forth into sobs, and cries, and convulsive raptures of "Glory! glory, Alleluja!"

Many visitors fall sick, and some die in the camp. In the agonies of this strife against the power of sin and the fear of death (I am told by men who have often watched these spiritual tempests) the passions seem to be all unloosed, and to go astray without let or guide. "I like to hear of a revival," said to me a lawyer of Indianapolis; "it brings on a crop of cases." In the revivalist camp men quarrel, and fight, and make love to their neighbours' wives. A Methodist preacher of twenty-five years' experience, first in New England, then on the frontiers, afterwards on the battle-fields of Virginia, said to me, "Religious passion includes all other passions; you cannot excite one without stirring up the others. In our Church we know the evil, and we have to guard against it as we may. The young men who get up revivals are always objects of suspicion to their elders; many go wrong, I would say one in twenty at the least; more, far more, than that number bring scandal on the Church by their thoughtless behaviour in the revivalist camps."

In a week, in a month, perhaps, the fire of religious zeal may begin to flicker and die down. Quarrels break out, and bowie-knives are drawn. The cynical laugh, the indifferent drive away.

Horses are now put up; waggons are laden with baggage and women; the publican strikes his tent; and the riff-raff goes in search of another field. One by one the brawlers are knocked off, until the marabout himself, disgusted with his hearers, ceases to give tongue. Then the last horse is saddled, the last cart is on the road, and nothing appears to have been left of that singular camp but a few burnt logs, a desecrated wood, and two or three freshly-made graves.

And is that all? The Shaker says, No. In the frenzies of that camp-meeting, he detects a moral order, a spiritual beauty, utterly unseen by secular eyes. To him, a revival is God's own method of calling His children to Himself. Without a revival, there can be no resurrection on a large and inclusive scale: — and no revival, it is said by him, is ever quite wasted to the human race. Some soul is always drawn by it into the peace of heaven.

Frederick told me that every great spiritual revival which has agitated America since his Church was planted, has led to a new society being founded on the principles of Mother Ann. The eighteen unions represent eighteen revivals. According to Elder Frederick, who is watching with a keen and pitying eye the vagaries of the new spiritualist movements in America, a nineteenth revival is now at hand, from the action of which he expects a considerable extension of his Church.

## CHAPTER XV.

#### Spiritualism.

During the past month of August, a crowd of Spiritualists has been holding conference in this picturesque port and peculiar city of Providence, Rhode Island.

The disciples came in troops from the east and the west; some being delegates from circles and cities, representing thousands who stayed at home; still more being disciples who scorned either to admit any rule or to express any one's opinions save their own. Eighteen States and Territories were represented on the platform by accredited members; more than half of them, it seems, by ladies. A first convention of Spiritualists, on a scale sufficiently vast to be called national, was held two years ago at Chicago; a second was held one year ago at Philadelphia; but in those two meetings, regarded by the zealous as experimental, the delegates came together less by choice than chance. Convenience of men and women, not moral significance, had ruled the selection of a place of meeting; but when a platform had been voted in Chicago, and a great appeal to the public had been made in Philadelphia, moral considerations came into play. The scene of the third National Convention of Spiritualists was fixed in this city, on account of the peculiar fame of Providence as a camp of heretics and reformers, — the refuge of Roger Williams, the home of religious toleration, the city of "What Cheer?"

Quiet observers of the scene were struck with the wild and intellectual appearance of this cloud of witnesses. 'Their eyes, I am told, were preternaturally bright; their faces preternaturally pale. Many of them practised imposition of hands. Nearly all the men wore long hair; nearly all the women were closely cropped.

Pratt's Hall in Broad Street was engaged for the sittings; a capacious chamber, though not too large for the crowd of angels and of mortals who came pressing in. Yes, angels and mortals. Elderess Antoinette is not more certain that she sees and hears the dead than are all these hirsute men. In Broad Street, angels stood in the doorway, spectres flitted about the room. Their presence was admitted, their sympathy assumed, and their counsel sought. A dozen times the speakers addressed their words, not only to delegates present in the flesh, but to heavenly messengers who had come to them in the spirit.

L. K. Joslin, a leader in the local circles, welcomed the delegates to this city of refuge, in their character of heretics and infidels. "'To-day," he said, addressing his mortal hearers, "the Spiritualists of the United States are the Great Heretics; and, *as such*, the Spiritualists of Providence greet you with their welcome, believing that you are infidel to the old heresies that cursed rather than blessed our whole humanity." These words appear to have been official; also what followed them, in reference to the celestial portion of his audience. "But not unto you alone," he said, with a solemn emphasis, "do we look for counsel, for inspiration, and the diviner harmonies. The congregation is greater than the seeming. There are others at the doors. Those of other ages, who were the morning lights to the world, fearless, true, and martyred in the earth-life for their devotion to the truth — the cherished wise and good of the long-ago, and the loved ones of the near past — they will manifest their interest in, and favour with their presence, the largest body of individuals on this continent who realize their actualized presence and power. And unto them, as unto you, we give the greeting." Loud applause, not hushed and reverent, I am told, responded to this welcome of the heavenly delegates.

John Pierpont, of Washington, an aged preacher, (once a student of Yale College — the school of American prophets), in yielding the chair which he had held at Philadelphia, spoke of the term Infidel as applied to himself and his brethren in the spirit. "I am infidel," he exclaimed, "to a great many of the forms of popular religion; because I do not believe in many of the points which are held by a majority of the Christians, nay, even of the Protestant Church." He went on to say, that instead of putting his faith in creeds and canons, he put it in progress, liberty, and spirits.

Ten days after Pierpont's delivery of this speech

the old man died; and in less than ten days after his funeral, Mrs. Conant, a Boston medium, who writes spirit-messages for half the American public, announced that she had got his soul back again in her drawing-room; a presence visible to her, sensible to some, audible to many. Charles Crowell and J. M. Peebles report that in their presence, Mrs. Conant fell into a spirit-trance, when the soul of John Pierpont passed into her (after the fashion set by Ann Lee), and spoke to them through her lips of that higher world into which he had just been raised. "It was evident," they say, "that some spirit was taking possession of her, for it portrayed its last earthly scene. The departure must have been very easy, for there was no struggle in the demonstration; merely a few short breathings, an earnest and steady gaze, and all was over. An effort was made to speak, and soon this immortal sentence was uttered: —

"'Blessed, thrice blessed, are they who die with a knowledge of the truth.'

"After a slight pause, the spirit resumed: —

"'*Brothers and Sisters*, the problem now is solved with me. And because I live, you shall live also; for the same *divine Father and Mother* that confers immortality upon one soul bestows the gift upon all.'"

Pierpont would not seem to have made much progress in celestial knowledge by the change from flesh to spirit; for while he was on earth he confined his arguments on spirit-rapping and spirit-writing very much to these forms: — "I have seen, and therefore I know; I have felt, and therefore I believe." It would seem to have struck Pierpont's spirit that his communication might be regarded as unsatisfactory to his mortal friends, seeing how warm a curiosity impels many of them to inquire into the mysteries of a higher world; and he spoke to Crowell and Peebles, through Mrs. Conant, in a tone of apology. "I regret," he is reported to have said, "that I cannot portray to you the transcendent beauty of the vision I saw just before I passed to the spirit-world. The glories of this new life are beyond description. Language would fail me should I attempt to describe them." Mortals had heard that language used before John Pierpont died.

When Pierpont left the chair, Newman Weeks, of Vermont, was elected president for the year. Among the vice-presidents were several ladies; Mrs. Sarah Horton of Vermont, Mrs. Deborah Butler of New Jersey, Doctoress Juliette Stillman of Wisconsin.

Warren Chace, of Illinois, one of the male vice-presidents, declares that more than three millions of Americans, men and women, have already entered into this movement. Three millions is a large figure; no church in these States, not even the Methodist, can sum up half that number of actual members. The Spiritualists count in their ranks some eminent men; shrewd lawyers, gallant soldiers, graceful writers; with not a few persons who can hardly escape the suspicion of being simply rogues and cheats. Still, the fact about them which concerns a student of the New America most is their reported strength in numbers. A society of three million men and women would be formidable in any country; in a republic governed by popular votes, they must wield an enormous force for either good or ill; hence, one is not surprised on finding their leaders boast of having power to control the public judgments of America, not only as to peace and war, dogma and practice, but even on the more delicate questions of social and moral life. A fair and open field is not to be refused when hosts so mighty throw down wager of battle on behalf of what they hold to be true, however strange their faith may seem.

These millions, more or less, of Spiritualists announce their personal conviction that the old religious gospels are exhausted, that the churches founded on them are dead, that new revelations are required by man. They proclaim that the phenomena, now being produced in a hundred American cities — signs of mysterious origin, rappings by unknown agents, drawings by unseen hands; phenomena which are commonly developed in darkened rooms and under ladies' tables — offer an acceptable ground-plan for a new, a true, and a final faith in things unseen. They have already their progressive lyceums, their catechisms, their newspapers; their male and female prophets, mediums, and clairvoyants; their Sunday services, their festivals, their pic-nic parties, their camp-meetings; their local societies, their state organisations, their general conferences; in short, all the machinery of our most active, most aggressive societies. Their strength may be put too high by Warren Chace; outsiders cannot count them, since they are not returned in the census as a separate body; but the number of their lyceums, the frequency of their pic-nics, the circulation of their journals, are facts within reach of some sort of verification. A man would hardly be wrong in assuming that a tenth part of the population in these New England States, a fifteenth part of the population of New York, Ohio, and Pennsylvania, lie open, more or less, to impressions from what they call the spirit-world.

Some of these zealots urge a most ancient origin for their faith, while others maintain that they are a new people, blessed with an unworn revelation, a growth of the American soil, an exclusive property of the American church. They allude but seldom to the Shakers, from whom they seem to have derived nearly all their canons, with not a few of their practices. They prefer to trace their origin to the visions of Andrew Jackson Davis and the happy audacities of Kate and Caroline Fox. A majority, perhaps, of the National delegates would have resented, as an injury to their country, any attempt to carry back the spiritual movement to an older source than the revelations of their own Poughkeepsie seer.

Poughkeepsie, pronounced Po'keepsie, the Mecca, the Benares, the Jerusalem, of this new church, is a green, though busy and thriving town, lying at the foot of a picturesque bluff on the river Hudson, midway from Albany to New York. Seen from the river, the place is quaint and Swiss-like, with its old quay, its bustling hotels, its rickety exchange. A bend in the stream, there five or six hundred yards in width, landlocks the river, so as to form, as it were, two pretty lakelets; the higher one backed by the Catskill mountains, the lower one by the Hudson highlands. The nearer bank is bare and weird; with rock above and scrub below; but the western shore, a rolling ridge of hill, is bright with sycamore, beech, and oak. Schools, churches, colleges, abound in the city; and among persons who have never been touched by unseen fingers, guns, carpets, beer, and cotton, are mentioned as its productions. Among the elect, the chief production of Po'keepsie is a Seer.

When Mother Ann had been lodged in the gaol of this river town, she had gathered a little court of curious people round her, to whom she communicated her strange experiences of the unseen world. Andrew Davis, the poor cobbler, is a spiritual descendant of Ann Lee, the poor factory girl. Davis sees signs and dreams dreams; but his revelations have scarcely gone beyond the hints afforded by Mother Ann. In his trances, he declares that in dying men only change their garments, that the spirits of the dead are about us everywhere, that sensitive persons can communicate with them. He asserts that medicines are useless and hurtful, and that all diseases may be cured by laying on of hands. He describes a new method of education, in which a sort of dancing with the arms and hands in Shaker fashion is largely introduced. He denounces the Christian Church as an institution of the flesh, the time of which has passed away, and he proposes in its stead a new and everlasting covenant of the spirit.

Such are, in brief, the bases of what Newman Weeks, Sarah Horton, Deborah Butler, and the associated brethren proclaimed in Pratt's Hall as that new covenant, which is to elevate man from the lowest earth into the highest heaven. Like Elder Frederick, they maintained the dual nature of the Godhead, assuming a female and a male essence — a Motherhood as well as Fatherhood in the Creator — and, like Sister Mary and Elderess Antoinette, they inferred from this duality of God the equal right and privilege of the sex on earth. Indeed, from first to last, the ladies seem to have played the leading parts in Providence, whether in exposition or in expostulation. There was much of both these articles. Miss Susie Johnson said she was tired of talk and wanted to work. "I am ready," cried the young reformer, "to work with any man or woman, or any community, that will show me the first practical step, by virtue of which we shall be laying the foundation of a higher morality, of a stricter integrity, of a better government, and, finally, of a higher destiny for the whole human race. I want to do something, and I want to see others who are ready to work. It is very much easier, I know, to pray for the salvation of mankind than to work for it, and oftentimes you get very much more credit for praying than for working; but it is not that I am after. I am sincerely devoted to the interests of the children of the coming generation."

Mrs. Susie Hutchinson was bolder still in rebuke of her brethren in the spirit. This lady, who represented the Charleston Independent Society of Spiritualists in the Convention, said she had laboured for eight years in the cause of Spiritualism, but had always been ashamed of her associates. The official report makes her say: "She had never met a whole-souled, noble Spiritualist yet, but she had hoped that there would be a class of people here who would show themselves worthy of being called men and women. She had hoped that they would pass resolutions that should be active, and not dead letters, going back to the buried past, and that they would find manhood and womanhood coming up to the work of humanity. If there was one single soul in the universe to be shut out from the convention, she wanted to be shut out with them. If there was a single person going to hell, she wanted to go with them; and if there was a work to be done in the lower regions, she would go and help the Eternal Father to do that work."

Not a few of the delegates pretended to the possession of miraculous powers; to the gift of tongues, to spiritual insight, to the art of healing. Nearly all the adepts undertake to cure diseases by imposition (scoffers say by very great imposition) of hands. In a current copy of 'The Banner of Light' you may count a score of male and female — mostly female — mediums, who publicly advertise to cure diseases of every kind — for due amount of dollars — by spirit-agencies; a certain virtue being conveyed from the physician to her patient, by a movement of the hands, in imitation of the apostolic rite. These announcements of the healing mediums are often curious and suggestive. Among lesser lights in these circles, Mrs. Eliza Williams, a sister of Andrew Jackson Davis, announces that she will "examine and prescribe for diseases and cure the sick by her healing powers, which have been fully tested." Mrs. S. J. Young advertises herself as a business and medical clairvoyant; Mrs. Spafford as a trance-test medium; Mrs. II. S. Seymour as a business and test medium. Some of these advertisements are full of mystery to the carnal mind. Mrs. Spencer undertakes to cure chills and fevers by her "positive and negative powders," adding, "for the prevention and cure of cholera this great spiritual medicine should be always kept on hand." Dr. Main, who dates from the Health Institute, requests those persons who may wish to have his opinion, to "enclose a dollar, a postage-stamp, and a 'lock of hair." Mrs. R. Collins "still continues to heal the sick in Pine Street." Madam Gale, clairvoyant and test medium, "sees spirits and describes absent friends." Mrs. H. B. Gillette, electric, magnetic, healing and developing medium, "heals both body and mind." But Mrs. GHlette appears to be distanced by Dr. George Emerson, who announces "a new development of spirit-power." This medium is "developed to cure diseases by drawing the disease into himself;" and he advertises that he is ready to perform this miracle of spirit-art by letter, at any distance, for ten dollars. In some respects, however, the ladies make a bolder show of might than anything yet assumed by the rougher sex. Mrs. S. W. Gilbert, describing herself as a Dermapathist, not only offers to cure disease, but to teach the art of curing it — in so many lessons, at so much a lesson!

A tone of stern hostility towards the religious creeds and moral standards of all Christian nations marked the speeches of men and women throughout this Convention; a tone which is hardly softened by a word in the official reports.

Miss Susie Johnson said, she for one would build no more churches, "for they had already too long oppressed and benighted humanity."

Mr. Andrew Foss "thanked God this was not an age of worship, but of investigation."

Dr. H. T. Child said that "Spiritualism has bridged the gulf between Abraham's bosom and the rich man's hell. Let thanksgiving be added to thanksgiving for every blow that is struck to weaken the superstructure of human law — law which, by the hand of man, punishes men for doing wrong."

Mr. Perry said, "As a Spiritualist, I have yet to learn that we hold anything as sacred, and I am opposed to any resolution that has the word sacred in it."

Mr. Finney said, "The old religion is dying out. We are here to represent this new religion, born of the Union and of the types of humanity in a cosmopolitan geography, the die of which was cast in the forges of Divine Providence."

This was, in fact, the substance of what was said in presence of the assembled delegates, mortal and celestial, at the third National Convention.

Three resolutions were adopted, which the Spiritualists consider as of great importance. The first was, to oppose the teaching of Sunday-schools and to substitute for it that of their own progressive Lyceums: the second, to procure the writing of a series of essays on Spiritualism: the third, to discountenance the use of tobacco and strong drinks. A proposal to found a National Spiritual College was ordered to stand over for discussion next year. One resolution, of no immediate impulse, showed how broad an action might be taken by these Spiritualists on the political field, if they should gain in strength of numbers and in unity of purpose. It referred to the Labour question, and ran as follows: —

"Resolved, That the hand of honest labour alone holds the sovereign sceptre of civilisation; that its rights are commensurate with its character and importance; and hence, that it should be so fully and completely compensated as to furnish to the toiling millions ample means, times, and opportunities for education, culture, refinement, and pleasure; and that equal labour, whether performed by men or women, should receive equal compensation."

These reformers pay no respect to our Old World notions of political science.

When we essay to judge a system so repugnant to our feelings, so hostile to our institutions, as this school of Spiritualism, it is needful — if we would be fair in censure — to remember that, strange as it may seem to on-lookers, it has been embraced by hundreds of learned men and pious women. Such a fact will appear to many the most singular part of the movement; but no one can assert that a theory is simply foolish, beneath the notice of investigators, which has been accepted by men like Judge Edmonds, Dr. Hare, Elder Frederick, and Professor Bush.

## CHAPTER XVI.

#### Female Seers.

In this learned, bright, and picturesque city of Boston, the home of Agassiz, Longfellow, Holmes, and Lowell, there has risen up a branch of the female priesthood of America, which puts forward a claim to regulate science, to supersede induction, and to lay down a new method. The women are Female Seers.

These priestesses, who may be called Elizabethans, from the name of their founder and hierophant, Elizabeth Denton, are not, properly speaking, a church; hardly indeed a sect; and certainly not a learned society. Perhaps they may be called a school; since they profess to have everything to learn and everything to teach. Like most other branches of the great Spiritualist family, they live in the world, of which they enjoy the pleasures and covet the distinctions with unflagging zest. On Boston Common, they are undistinguishable by outward signs from the world of ordinary people (if, in truth, it can be said that on Boston Common there are any ordinary people). Their mark is that of an inward, intellectual gift; the peculiar power of these Female Seers being the ability to read into the very heart of millstones.

Obeying the common law of these new societies,

the school of Elizabeth is a female school, with ladies for its prophets and interpreters. Men may become members of the school; may share in its riches, help to propagate its gospels; but no male creature has ever yet dared to assert his possession of its miraculous gifts.

In our new philosophy, superior gifts depend on superior organisation. Man, with his coarser grain, his harder fibre, his duller spirit, is unequal to the flights and ecstasies of the nobler sex. In New York idiom, man has been played out, and woman must have her turn.

Anne Cridge began it. Anne Cridge is a sister of William Denton, of Boston, a person of some consequence here — for a man; a student, a geologist, a collector, one who can chop logic and quote authorities in defence of the doings of his school. The new Gospel of the Female Seers came to Anne Cridge and her brother William in this odd manner. Buchanan, a doctor in Cincinnati, had noticed in his practice, that some persons can be purged without pills and doses, simply by being made to hold the cathartic medicine in their hands. It was an act of the imagination; not to be expected from every one, perhaps, but certainly to be found in some; especially in females of delicate genius and of sensitive frame. Why not in Anne Cridge? The delicate genius, the sensitive frame, were hers by nature and not by choice. A trial was made. Now, a fancy that could supply the place of a bolus should be capable of higher service than purging the body of its viler humours; and with a sly feminine frankness, Anne tried her powers of seeing through obstacles on some of her friends' unopened letters. The gift soon grew upon her. Putting a sealed paper to her temples, she perceived traces upon it, not with her eyes, but with her brain, of the figure of a man writing, — the figure of the man who had written that paper, — so that she could tell his height, his colour, and the shape of his eyes. A thought now struck her brother. This image of a man writing must be a sun-picture, which had been thrown upon the paper, as upon a lens. He could not himself see it; only his sister Anne could see it; but this defect of vision was a consequence of his grosser qualities of mind. Denton lacked imagination. Still, it was made clear to him, that Nature must be in the daily habit of multiplying pictures of herself; that every surface must receive and may retain such pictures; and that you only want a seer capable of reading them, in order to arrive at Nature's innermost secrets. It was a fine idea; Denton thought the beginning of a new era: for if Anne, by pressing a piece of paper against her forehead, could find on it the figure of its writer, with an outline of the room in which it had been folded and sealed, why should she not be able to read the images which must have been pictured on all other surfaces; on flints, on bones, on shells, on metals? Why not? If the images mirrored on all substances by light, are not, as we fancy, transient, but remain upon them, sinking into them, it is simply a question of test — of an agent sensitive enough to perceive and recover these vanishing lines. Such an agent Denton had found in his sister Anne.

Having found his reader of Nature, all the past life of the world would be opened to him, as one great fragment of time is to the Wandering Jew, with the added advantage that he could go further back in time and could read the things which no human eyes had ever seen. To wit, if his theory were true, you would only need to break a piece of rock from the Matterhorn, wrap it in paper, and place it against the reader's brow, in order to learn, as from the pages of a book, the story of the glaciers, from the age when Switzerland and Swabia were fields of ice, through the melting periods, down to the day when forest, lake, town, vineyard, laughed upon the scene; to scratch a flint from the limestone quarries of the White Mountain, and you would find engraved upon it pictures of the primæval forest, of the Indian camp, the red-skins in their paint and feathers, brandishing their spears, and tossing in their war-dance; to pick a bit of lava from a vault in Pompeii, and you would obtain a map of the Italian city, with its houses, gardens, baths and circuses, its games, its festivals, its civic and religious life; to chip a scale from the tower of Seville, and you would instantly restore the old Moorish life of that proud city, with its ensigns and processions, its dusk population, its gleaming crescents and heroic pomp of war; to snatch a bone from a heap of sailors' ballast lying on the quays, and mayhap you would have pictured on this fossil the condition of England thousands of years before Cæsar sailed from the Somme, with portraits of the savages who fished, and fought, and fed goats and sheep on our shores and downs. If the theory were only true, a new light had dawned upon the world; history had obtained a great supplement, science a new basis, art a fresh illustration.

But Anne, the first Female Seer, now found a rival in this art of reading stones in Elizabeth Denton, her brother's wife. It may be that Elizabeth was jealous of Anne passing day after day in her husband's study, even though it were only among books, bones, skins, and ores, gazing with him into the mysteries of life, while she herself was sent out into the nursery and the kitchen. In her eyes, it is probable that in such services to science one woman would seem to be as good as another — in her own case a great deal better. Certain it is, that she one day told her husband that she, too, was a Female Seer, able and willing to look for him into the soul of things. Denton tried her with a pebble, which she instantly read off in a fashion to extinguish the modest pretensions of sister Anne. In the published list of experiments, we are told that a piece of limestone from Kansas, full of small fossil shells, was held by Anne Cridge against her brow, when she read off: "A deep hole here. What shells! small shells; so many. I see water; it looks like a river running along." The next experiment was tried upon Elizabeth: a bit of quartz from Panama being held before her eyes: "I see what looks like a monstrous insect; its body covered with shelly wings, and its head furnished with antennæ nearly a foot long. It stands with its head against a rock . . . I see an enormous snake coiled up among wild, wiry grass. The vegetation is tropical." "Well done!" cried Denton.

Proud of the gifts so suddenly displayed by his wife, he announced that a new science had been seen, a new interpretation of the past revealed, and opening a fresh page in the great book of nature, he wrote down the word Psychometry, by which he meant the Science of the Soul of things. Of course, being only a male, he cannot show this soul to others; he does not affect to see it for himself. He is privileged through his sister and his wife. But being a man of letters and ideas, he has shaped out the new mystery of the universe in these surprising terms: —

"In the world around us radiant forces are passing from all objects to all objects in their vicinity, and during every moment of the day and night are daguerreotyping the appearances of each upon the other; the images thus made not merely resting upon the surface, but sinking into the interior of them; there held with astonishing tenacity, and only waiting for the suitable application to reveal themselves to the inquiring gaze. You cannot, then, enter a room by night or day, but you leave on going out your portrait behind you. You cannot lift your hand, or wink your eye, or the wind stir a hair of your head, but each movement is infallibly registered for coming ages. The pane of glass in the window, the brick in the wall, and the paving-stone in the street, catch the pictures of all the passers-by, and faithfully preserve them. Not a leaf waves, not an insect crawls, not a ripple moves, but each motion is recorded by a thousand faithful scribes in infallible and indelible scripture."

It is a pity that men are not allowed to see these pictures, to read these histories, of our globe. But the male vision is dull, the male mind prosaic. Only the female sense can peer into these solid depths. It is rather hard upon us; but whose fault is it if man's grosser nature cannot soar to these feminine heights?

Growing by what it feeds on, the mysterious faculty in Elizabeth Denton has left that of Anne Cridge immeasurably behind. She has acquired the gift of looking, not into flints and fossils only, but into the depths of the sea, into the centre of the earth. She can hear the people of past times talk, she can taste the food which saurians and crustaceans scrunched in the pre-diluvian world.

From these Female Seers we have learnt that men were once like monkeys; that even then the women were in advance of men; being less hairy and standing more erect than their male companions. It is coming to be always thus, when the story of man's life is told by a properly qualified female saint and seer.

## CHAPTER XVII.

#### Equal Rights.

"ARE you a member of the Society for Promoting Equal Rights, as between the two sexes?" I asked a young married lady of my acquaintance in New York. "Certainly not," she replied with a quick shrug of the shoulders. "Why not?" I ventured to say, pursuing my inquiry. "Oh," she answered, with a sly little laugh, "you see I am very fond of being taken care of." Were it not for this fortunate weakness on the part of many ladies, the Society for Promoting Equal Rights would soon, I am told, comprise the whole female population of these states, especially of these New England states!

The reform which ladies like Betsey Cowles, Lucy Stone, and Lucretia Mott, would bring about by way of equalising the rights of sex and sex, would give to woman everything that society allows to men, from pantaloons and latch-keys up to seats in the legislature and pulpits in the church. In assertion of female rights, Harriet Noyes and Mary Walker have taken to pantalettes; Elizabeth Stanton has offered herself as a candidate for the representation of New York; and Olympia Brown has been duly ordained as a minister of the gospel.

When the first Female Congress was called in Ohio, under Presidentess Betsey Cowles, the ladies, after much reading and speaking, adopted twenty-two resolutions, with a preamble echoing the form of the Declaration of Independence: —

"Whereas all men are created equal, and endowed with certain God-given rights, and all just government is derived from the consent of the governed; And whereas the doctrine that man shall pursue his own substantial happiness, is acknowledged by the highest authority to be the great precept of nature; And whereas this doctrine is not local but universal, being dictated by God Himself: Wherefore . . . ."

Then come the resolutions, which take the form of an open declaration, that the ladies of Ohio shall in future consider the laws which, in their opinion, press unfairly on the sex, as of no effect and void.

"1. Resolved: That all laws contrary to these fundamental principles, or in conflict with this great precept of nature, are of no binding obligation.

"2. Resolved: That all laws which exclude women from voting are null and void.

"3. Resolved: That all social, literary, pecuniary, and religious distinctions between man and woman are contrary to nature.

"9. Resolved: That it is unjust and unnatural to hold a different moral standard for men and for women."

Lydia Pierson put her foot down on what she held to be the true cause of female inferiority: the habit among girls of marrying early in life. Lydia told her audience that, if they wanted to be men they must stay at school until they were twenty-one.

Massachusetts — the true leader in every movement of opinion — now took up the question, and the first National Woman's Rights Convention was held in Worcester, with Paulina Davis, of Rhode Island, Presidentess, and Hannah Darlington, of Pennsylvania, Secretary.

Paulina described the object of that female parliament to be — an epochal movement, the emancipation of a class, the redemption of half the world, the re-organisation of *all* social, political, and industrial interests and institutions. She said, This is the age of peace, and woman is its sign. The Congress voted the following resolutions: —

"That every human being of full age, who has to obey the law, and who is taxed to support the government, should have a vote:

"That political rights have nothing to do with sex, and the word 'male' should be struck out of all our state constitutions:

"That the laws of property, as affecting married persons, should be revised, so as to make all the laws equal; the wife to have during life an equal control over the property gained by their mutual toil and sacrifices, to be heir of her husband to the extent that he is her heir, and to be entitled at her death to dispose by will of the same share of the joint property as he is."

Other resolutions declared the right of women to a far better education than they now enjoy, to a fair partnership with men in trade and adventure, and to a share in the administration of justice. A male listener said he liked the spirit of this female parliament, since he found they meant by woman's rights the right of every lady to be good for something in life!

One topic of discourse in this Congress was Dress. It would hardly be outstripping facts to say that the husk and shell, so to speak, of every question now being raised for debate in America, as between sex and sex, belongs to the domain of the milliner and the tailor. What are the proper kinds of clothes for a free woman to fold about her limbs? Is the gown a final form of dress? Is the petticoat a badge of shame? Does a man owe nothing to his hat, his coat, his pantaloons, his boots? In short, can a female be considered as equal to a male until she has won the right to wear his garb? Queries such as these have a serious as well as comic side. Feminine science is so far advanced in these countries, that many a topic which would be food for jokes and poesies in London, is treated here as a question of business would be considered in a Broadway store.

Now dress, if you consider it apart from the rules of Hyde Park and Fifth Avenue, denotes something other than the personal taste of its wearer. Dress is the man; and something more. Dress not only tells you what a man does, but what he is. Watch the tide of life, as it flows and surges through the Broadway, past the Park, the Battery, and the Quays, and you will see that the preacher has one costume, the postman another, the sailor a third; that the man of easy habit clothes himself in a garb which a man of swift and decisive movements could not wear. A flowing garment impedes the owner; a man or woman in skirts cannot run like a fellow in pantaloons.

Helene Marie Weber was one of the first to don coat and trousers, and her assumption of male attire was a cause of loud explosions. Helene, besides being a writer on reform, on female education, and on dress, was a practical farmer, who ploughed land, sowed corn, reared pigs, and went to market with her produce, habited like a man, in boots, breeks, and buttons. Apart from this fancy, she is described as a strictly pious and lady-like person, modest in mien, unassuming in voice. In a letter which she wrote to the Ladies' Congress, she mentions that she had been abused in the English and American papers for wearing trousers; she declares that she has no desire to be an Iphis; that she never affected to be other than a woman, and has never been mistaken for a man except by some hasty stranger. Her common garb she describes as consisting of a coat and pants of black cloth; her evening dress as a dark blue coat with gilt buttons, buff cassimere vest, richly trimmed, with gold buttons, and drab breeches. She adds, with a sweet feminine touch, that all her clothes are made in Paris!

Many of the points to which these ladies lent their countenance were of serious import; others were only noticeable for the comedy to which they gave birth. I have heard that a deputation of ladies in one of these New England towns went up to their minister's house to protest against the commencement of the daily lessons with the words, "Dearly beloved brethren," as implying that the women were either not present or counted for nothing in the congregation. They wished to have their pastor's views on a project for amending the Book of Common Prayer. "Well, I have thought over that matter, ladies," said the preacher; "but I think, on the whole, this text may stand; for you see the brethren always embrace the sisters."

The more serious question discussed in the Equal Rights Association is the position of woman in marriage. "The whole theory of the common law," they say, "in relation to the married woman is unjust and degrading." What, they ask, are the natural relations of one sex to the other? Is marriage the highest and purest form of those relations? What are the moral effects of marriage upon man and wife? Is marriage a holy state?

Any appeal to the code for guidance on such questions would be idle; for the rule under which we live has no reply to make in matters of moral and religious truth. The Institutes, Pagan alike in origin and in spirit, consider a woman as little more than a chattel; and the relation of husband and wife as only a trifle more advanced than that of a master and his slave. They see no moral beauty in the state of marriage; see nothing in it beyond a partnership in family business, akin to that which exists in a trading firm. No Roman ever dreamt of love being divine, of marriage being a union of two souls; and this Gothic sentiment, so common in our poetry, in our traditions, in our households, finds no food whatever in the civil law. Hence it has come to pass in America, that every sect of social reformers — Moravian, Tunker, Shaker, Perfectionist, Mormon, Spiritualist — has commenced its efforts towards a better life by discarding and denouncing the civil law.

That the state of marriage is the highest, most poetic, most religious stage of the social relations, is denied by few, even in America. It is denied by some. The Moravians and the Tunkers treat the institution with a certain shyness; not denying that for carnal persons it is a good and profitable state; but affecting to believe that it is not holy, not conducive to the highest virtue. The Shakers, we have seen, repudiate marriage altogether, as one of those temporal institutions which have done their appointed office on this earth, and have now passed away, so far, at least, as concerns the elected children of grace.

## CHAPTER XVIII.

### The Harmless People.

THE Tunkers, who say they came into America from a small German village on the Oder, all from one little dorf, owe the name by which they are known, not only here, in Lancaster, Pennsylvania, about which they are largely settled, but in Boston and New York — to a pun. They profess Baptist tenets; and the word "tunker" meaning to dip a crumb into gravy, a sop into wine, they are described by those who use it, in a very poor joke, as dippers and sops. They are also called Tumblers, from one of the abrupt motions which they make in the act of baptism. We English style them Dunkers, by mistake. Among themselves they are known as Brethren; the spirit of their association being that of fraternal love. The name by which they are known in the neighbourhood of their villages in Pennsylvania, Ohio, and Indiana, is that of the Harmless People.

Under any and every name, they are a sober, pious, and godly race; leavening with a simple virtue the mighty fermentations going forward on the American soil.

These Tunkers live in little villages and groups of farms, for their common comfort and advantage; but not in separate communities, like the Shakers and Perfectionists. They remain in the world, subject to the law. In some respects, they may be considered as in a state of change, even of decay; for, in these later days, they have begun to take interest on money lent, once strictly forbidden among them; and they have commenced to build chapels and churches instead of confining their religious services, like the ancient Jews, to houses and sheds. In some of these chapels, I am sorry to say, there is even a hint at decoration; but with these slight drawbacks, the Tunkers are true to the practices of their faith, of which these brief particulars may be given.

They are said to believe that all men will be saved; a dogma which is common to almost every new sect in the United States; though some of their body deny that universal salvation is held as a binding article of their creed. They dress in plain clothes, and use none but the simplest forms of address. They swear no oaths. They make no compliments. They will not fight. They wear long beards, and never go to law. In their worship they employ no salaried priest. Males and females are considered equals, and the two sexes are alike eligible for the diaconate. Every man in a congregation is allowed to rise (as in the Jewish synagogue) and expound the text; the man who proves himself ablest to teach and preach is put in the minister's place; but the people pay him in respect, not in dollars, for his service. Like Peter and Paul on their travels, the Tunker apostles may be lodged with their brethren, and even helped on their way with food and gifts; but both in theory and in practice they accept no fees, even when they happen to be poor and unable to leave for a week, for a month, without loss, their little patches of ground. These unpaid preachers wait upon the sick, comfort the dying, bury the dead. They have also to marry young men and maids; a few, not many, of the more carnal spirits; a duty which is often the most troublesome part of their daily toils.

For the Tunkers, like the Essenes whom they resemble in many strong points, have peculiar views about the holiness of a single life; holding celibacy in the highest honour; and declaring that very few persons are either gifted or prepared for the married state. They do not refuse to bind any brother and sister who may wish to enter into that bond to each other; but they make no scruple about pointing out to them, in long and earnest discourse, the superior virtues of a single life. The preacher does not say that matrimony is a crime; he only hints a profound dislike to it; treating it as one of those evil things from which he would willingly guard his flock.

When a brother and sister come to him wanting to be made one flesh, he looks down upon them as sinners who ought to be questioned and probed as to their secret thoughts; and, if it may be, delivered by him through grace from a terrible snare. He alarms them by his inquisition, he frightens them by his prophecies. In his words and in his looks he conveys to their minds the idea that in wanting to be married they are going headlong to the devil. It is not easy to say what the object of these Harmless

People may be in opposing the tendency of their folks to love and marry; for the Tunkers are shy of publication and explanation; but it is open to conjecture that their motives may be partly physiological, partly religious. A wise man, who could have his way in every city of the world, would put an end to all marriages of deformed and idiotic persons; on the same lines of justification, a Tunker might dissuade from marriage a pair of lovers who could do nothing to improve the race. But some mystic dream, about chastity being a holy state, acceptable as such to God, and meritorious in the eyes of men, has more to do with it, I think, than any consideration they may have for improvements in the Tunker breed.

Of course, the Tunker body is not the first professing Christian Church which has felt it a duty to encourage people to live a single life, though the fact of such encouragement may be considered as having a meaning in a country, where every child is a fortune, which it never can have had in Europe and in Asia, where the separation of a great many monks and anchorites from the reproducing classes may have been justified on economical, if not on moral, grounds.

In the Churches of Jerusalem, Antioch, and Rome, the question of whether celibacy was or was not a holy state, was mooted long and freely, for apostles could be quoted on either side in the dispute, and the teachers, each according to his argument, might cite on this side the example of Peter, on that side the precept of Paul. The sentiment in favour of living a single life did not come from Paul, much less from Christ; it had sprung up among the Essenic farms and villages of Judea; had spread from the hill-side into the city and the schools; had become popular among the Pharisees, as a protest against the flesh and the devil; and, in this sense only, it appears to have been adopted by the ascetic Saul. After his conversion to a new creed, Paul, being a man of mature age, going to and fro in the world on his Master's work, was unlikely to change his habits. The spirit of the Essene was strong in Paul, but in pleading for chastity of the body, as a condition acceptable to God, it should not be hastily assumed that he set up his voice, even by implication, against God's own ordinance of marriage. Those only who have studied the social life of Corinth under Junius Gallio, — a sink of vice, appalling even to men most knowing in the ways of degenerate Greece, — can guess what may have been the apostle's motive for advising his disciples in that city to observe a more ascetic rule than any which they saw in vogue around them; but any man of sense may judge from the sacred text how far a special state of morals, special even among the Greeks, must have driven St. Paul into urging upon the Church of Corinth a true and resolute watchfulness over matters not otherwise recommended by him to the infant church. When he says to them, he would to God they were as he is, he speaks (if I read him rightly) as a chaste man rather than as a single man. How could an apostle of such practical and commanding genius as St. Paul conceive the idea of banishing marriage from the new society? Three reasons forbid it, any one of which would have been strong enough to deter him; (first) because Elohim, the God of his fathers, had instituted marriage for Adam and all his seed; (second) because Paul knew, and said, that if men do not marry, they will do much worse; and (third) because the rule of abstinence, if it could have been enforced by him, would have destroyed in one generation all his converts, and with them, perhaps, the very Church of Christ.

Have we any right to infer from Paul's advice to the Corinthians, that he held the views of Ann Lee, or even of Alexander Mack? Greece was not America; the Syrian Aphrodite is not worshipped in New York. St. Paul had to urge the merits of chastity on a people to whom that word, and all that it expresses, were unknown. His converts had been worshippers of Astarte, and in denouncing their abominations, he used the fiery freedom of a man whose life was pure and stainless. Yet he weighed his words, and in the tempest of his wrath took time to say, when he spoke in his own name only, as a private man, and when he delivered counsel in the name of our Lord. The Greeks understood him. Writing in their idiom, speaking of their manners, both well known to him — child of a Greek city, pupil in a Greek school — his meaning must have been clearer to them than it is to strangers. Hence the Greek church may be taken as a safer guide to the sense of a difficult and contested passage than any other, especially than that of the American

Tunker. The Greek church has no doubt about it. By many canons and by constant usage, that church affirms that St. Paul was in favour of wedlock, not in the communicant only, but in the priest.

Unhappily for Christian unity, the Western church took another view of the text. The Pauline and Platonic Fathers wrote in mystical phrases of the superior sanctity of an unmarried life; and long before any law of the church had come to forbid priest and bishop to marry, it had become a fashion among the higher clergy to abstain, and to live, as they phrased it, for the church alone. Strange to say, this fashion took root in Rome, in the midst of a people boasting as their chief glory, of having had for their founder and bishop St. Peter, Prince of the Apostles, a married man.

The adoption of this celibate principle by Rome was the germ of both the great schisms in the Christian society; first, of a parting between East and West, afterwards, in the West itself, of a parting between North and South. Disputes about dogma may be set aside; disputes about social order may not. A priest can be persuaded to hear reason on such topics as election and foreknowledge, who cannot be induced to admit that marriage is a state of sin. In the sixth and seventh centuries this battle of celibacy had been fiercely fought, the Petrine church being for it, the Pauline church against it; and on this rock of contradictions, the first great Christian society had struck and split. The Council of Tours had suspended for a year all priests and deacons who were then found living with their wives, of whom there were many thousands in Italy, Gaul, and Spain. The Council of Constantinople had declared that priests and deacons ought to live with their wives like laymen, according to the ordinance and custom of the apostles, a canon which they still observe. Not only did the Greek Church separate from that of Rome on this cardinal policy, but the clergy and laity of the West and North — of England, Germany, and France — stood out against it; and the main efforts of the Roman Church for five hundred years were given to this domestic question. Ages elapsed before Rome had crushed the opposition to her policy in England, Germany, and France, in which countries married priests were to be found so late as the times of the Black Prince: at length she won her cause; but on the morrow of her triumph the Reformation began.

No man can read the ballads and chronicles from Piers Ploughman's Complaint to Pecock's Repressor, without feeling how much it was beyond the power of a celibate clergy to dwell in peace with a congregation of Gothic race. The cry for a married priesthood rose from every corner of the West and North; and when the clerical reformers took the field against Rome, the first pledge of their sincerity, given and taken, was to marry wives. All the great men who led the Reformation in their several countries — Luther, Calvin, Cranmer — had to give this pledge of their faith; thus the newly-made Christian societies of North and West, to which America is heir, were founded on the broadest principles of human nature, not on the narrowest criticism of a text.

But Rome, after these great schisms in the church, clings fondly to her ancient order. She looks on woman as a snare. Into the crypt of St. Peter (a married saint) no female is allowed to enter, except on a single day of the year. A lady may not call upon the Pope, except in mourning robes. In the Roman mass no music is permitted for the female voice. But the Italian Church is logical in its practice, though it may be wrong in its principle. Where it is considered sinful in a priest to marry, how can you prevent the female being despised?

This question may be put to the American celibate schools: to the Tunkers of Ohio, to the Shakers of New York.

## CHAPTER XIX.

#### The Revolt of Woman.

Elizabeth Denton, founder though she be of a school of Female Seers, is not the highest and boldest of these feminine reformers. One school of writers, a school which is already a church, with its codes and canons, its seers and sects, soars high above local wranglings, into what is said to be a region of yet nobler truths. Rights of Woman! exclaim the party. What is right compared with power? what is usage compared with nature? what is social law compared with celestial fact? A woman's right to love, say these female reformers, is a detail, her claim to labour a mistake. Neither the first nor the second should be urged on the world's attention. One ought to be assumed, the other must be dropt. Woman's right to love is implied in a yet larger claim, and by the new theory of her life her only relation to labour is to be exempt from it.

These reformers make no feint, they hit straight out. According to them, only meek and weak reformers would think of prating about equal powers and laws. Women, they say, are not the equals of man; they are his superiors. They do not ask from him either chivalry or courtesy; they claim the sovereign rule. In throwing down such a gage, they are well aware how much they surprise and offend their masculine hearers; but they speak to women, and do not expect that men will receive the truth. They have a gospel to deliver, a duty to discharge, a war to conduct; a social war; no more, no less. Up to this time, they allege that women have been held in bondage; but their day has come, their chains are falling off, a deliverer is at hand; a truce, they cry, to compliments, to hypocrisies, to concessions on all sides; the movement now on foot is a Revolt of Woman against Man.

The first principle of this new party is, that of the two sexes Woman is the more perfect being, later in growth, finer in structure, grander in form, lighter in type. The distinctions between the two are wide and deep, one being allied to cherub and seraph, the other to stallion and dog. What man is to the gorilla, woman is to man. Female superiority is not confined to a few degrees of more or less; it is radical, organic, lying in the quality of her brain, in the delicacy of her tissues: a superiority of essence, even more than of grade. If nature works, as it would seem, through an ascending series, woman is the step beyond man in Nature's ascent towards the form of angelic life. And this is true, not only of human beings, but of all beings, from the female mollusk to the New England lady. Man is but the paragon of animals, while woman, by her gifts of soul, belongs to the celestial ranks. He is a lord of the earth, while she is a messenger from heaven.

The sexes, too, according to this female creed, differ in office, as they differ in endowment. Man is here to be a tiller of the soil, while his sister, nursed at the same breast, is meant for a prophetess and seer. One is made coarse and rough, that he may wrestle with the outward world; the other tender and douce, that she may commune with the spiritual spheres. Each sex, then, has a province of its own, in which the whole of its duty lies. Man has to work, woman to love. He labours with the flesh, she with the spirit. A husband is a grower and getter, his wife is a giver and spender; not in the way of jest and caprice, but by the eternal settlement of law. Man has to toil and save, that woman may dispense and enjoy; the higher intelligence turning his material gifts into use and beauty; as warmth draws wine and oil, colour and perfume, from the watered field. One sex is a cultivator, the other a reconciler. He deals with the lower, she with the higher aspects of nature. Man conquers the soil, Woman mediates with God.

The Prophetess of this new church is Eliza Farnham, of Staaten Island; the temple is unbuilt, but the faith and the votaries are said to be found in every populous city of the United States.

Five-and-twenty years have elapsed since the Truth of Woman first flashed upon Eliza; then a poor girl, unmarried, unlettered, untravelled, like most of these female seers; having read but little, speaking no tongue save one; yet keen and shrewd, with thoughts in her brain, and words upon her lips. This Truth of Woman came upon her in 1842, the year in which it is said that Joseph Smith received a command from God to restore plurality of wives;

came upon her, not by induction, but by intuition; in plainer words, she drew her dogma of superiority, as Smith drew his dogma of plurality, not from any facts in nature, but from the depths and riches of her mind. Like Smith, she either kept the secret to herself, or shared it only with her chosen friends. But women, she confesses, can teach each other fast, and her ideas were spread abroad by an unseen agency. When the Truth came upon her, she was yet a virgin; to prove its power, she married, becoming in turn a wife, a mother, a widow; making money and losing it; toiling with her hands for bread; burying her children as she had buried her husband; wandering from town to town, and from state to state; living upon other people's bounty; getting past the turn of a woman's life; watching the grey hairs start upon her head, the crow's feet pucker at her eyes; and then, with the evening shadows falling sadly on her life, having felt the joys and griefs of womanhood in all its phases, she was ready to begin the war, not secretly, and in other names, but with her principles avowed and her forces in the field.

The Revolt of Woman opened, as it ought to have opened, with an attack on pure Intellect: a faculty which the world, in its folly and injustice, puts above woman's susceptibilities and inspirations. Reason is man's stronghold; a fortress which he has built for himself, and in which he dwells alone. Yes; reason is the basis on which he has planted all those canons, systems, poetries, sciences, mythologies, which he turns with such deadly art against the partner of his life. But when Eliza came to look into this pure Intellect, what did she find? A high power, a divine faculty, a test of nature, an instrument of truth? Nothing of the kind. She saw in Intellect nothing more than a coarse bungler, dealing with nature in a slow, material way, gathering up a few dates and facts, tracing out causes and sequents, catching through harmonies at law. What was man's gift compared against woman's grace? A process against a power. A woman has no need of method. She knows the fact when she sees it, feels the truth when it is unseen. What man with his logic, observation and procedure, toils up to in a generation, she perceives at once. To him, intellect is a tiresome and uncertain guide; to her, intuition is a swift, unfailing diviner's rod. Has not man, asked Eliza, been using his reason for ages past, without having fallen on the central truth of life — the natural sovereignty of the female sex? Reason may have its uses and duties, of a humble kind; since it may teach a man how to cut down trees, how to build boats, how to snare game, how to reap corn and sow potatoes, how to fence his field and protect his camp; and for these uses it may be kept for a little while; but only in its proper place, as the servant of woman's far higher will.

The reign of Science was announced as over, that of Spiritualism as begun. Science is the offspring of man, Spiritualism of woman. The first is gross and sensual, a thing of the past; the second, pure and holy, a thing of the future. Science doubts, Spiritualism believes; one is of earth, the other is of heaven. Now that the Gospel of Woman is declared, Science has ceased to have a leading part in the discovery of truth; the objective world is about to pass into the subjective, and the superior sex will read for us, by their inner light, the mysteries of heaven and hell.

Eliza had no special theology to teach. She rejected Peter and Paul, Luther and Cranmer; but she had faith in Swedenborg. Peter and Paul had put women under men.

Eliza proudly contended that although her Truth of Woman is new and strange, it admits of proof convincing to the female mind. As to the masculine mind, a thing of lower grade, she was not concerned about its ways. A Virginian never thought of arguing with his slave. The Truth, which she had to preach, did not require man's sanction to make it pass; and she confined her discourse to the superior sex.

Her evidence in favour of the Truth of Woman lay in the following syllogism:—

Life is exalted in proportion to its organic and functional complexity; woman's organism is more complex, and her totality of functions larger, than those of any other being inhabiting our earth; therefore her position in the scale of life is the most exalted—the sovereign one.

That was Eliza's secret. The most complex life is the highest; woman's life is the most complex; ergo, woman's life is the highest. If the premises are sound, the conclusion must be also sound. Eliza felt so sure of her syllogism, that she rested her case upon it. What she claimed for woman is only what Nature gives her — the sovereign place.

It is the same, says Eliza, through all the animal grades. The females have more organs than the male, and organs are the representatives of power. All females have the same organs as males with two magnificent sets of structure which males have not; structures which concern the nourishing of life. She admits that the male is often physically larger than the female, so far as size can be measured by bulk of body, by length of arm, and by width of chest; but in lieu of any argument to be drawn from such a fact in favour of the male, it is urged that he is only bigger in the grosser parts — in bones and sinews — not in nerves and brains. Where the higher functions come into play, woman is in advance of man. Her bust has a nobler contour, her bosom a finer swell. The upper half of her skull is more expansive. All the tissues of her body are softer and more delicate. Her voice is sweeter, her ear quicker. Her veins are of brighter blue, her skin is of purer white, her lips are of deeper red. More than all else, as fixing the grade of woman above that of man, her brain is of higher quality and of quicker growth.

On every side, then, says Eliza, the female bears away the bell. She is aware that an old saying, based on what may be seen in a wood, in a street, in a farm-yard, asserts the superior beauty, no less than the superior size, of the male animal. But she disputes the facts. It is true that nearly all male animals have a grander figure; that nearly all male birds have a brighter plumage than their mates; that in some species the males have special ornaments, such as the lion's mane and the pea-cock's tail; but these appearances, she contends, deceive the eye, while true beauty is always to be found in the female form. The lioness is nobler than the lion; the pea-hen statelier than the cock. The beauty of your dung-hill rooster lies in his feathers and his voice. Pluck him to the skin, and you will find that he has neither the softness nor the beauty of his female mates. But Eliza will not rest her argument for feminine superiority on birds; for sex in birds is something of a mystery to her; and for many reasons (chiefly because girls are called nightingales, doves, and wrens) she inclines to the belief that the feminine of our higher order answers to the masculine in birds.

All, therefore, that is best and brightest in the two beings — outward and inward — beauty to the eye, softness to the touch, music to the ear — the heart to love, the brain to guide — are developed in the female on a richer scale. On his side, man has little to recommend him beyond a brutal strength. In short, the picture which Eliza draws of man and woman is very much like that of Caliban and Miranda on their lonely rock.

In support of these views of nature, she appeals to history, poetry, science, and art; citing Cornelia and the Mother of the Gracchi (whom she describes as *two* noticeable Roman wives); cutting up Shakespeare for his low views and slavish pictures of women; pooh-poohing Bacon for his lack of true method and insight; braining Michael Angelo for his absence of all feminine grace. There is novelty in her appeal, and in the illustrations by which she supports it. Eliza declares that Cornelia *and* the Mother of the Gracchi were but "average mothers of a later time;" that Shakespeare says nothing of woman that is to her credit, or to his own. Portia, it is true, is sensible, courageous, brilliant, without vanity; but Eliza knows a hundred American women who are better than she. Imogen is pure and loving; but the man is to be pitied who does not "know a score or two of finer girls." Rosalind, Perdita, Ophelia, Beatrice, are fools, if pretty ones, in whom Eliza can see "little goodness save the emptiness of evil." Pious Cordelia, loving Constance, noble Isabella, how are ye fallen, stars of the morning! Darwin, too, though he is allowed to be excellent in speculation, gets beyond his depth when dealing with structure, missing his chance of falling upon the Truth of Woman. Strange, she thinks, how so good a naturalist as Darwin is, should have treated rudimentary organs in male animals as remains of lost powers, when it is clear to her that they are the germs of new powers. But so it is; Darwin considers the rudimentary mammæ as the ruins of old organs, which once had uses; in other words, that male functions were at some distant period in the past a little nearer to female functions than they stand at present. Eliza, on the contrary, conceives that these mammæ are the germs of new organs, growing with the growth of time; in other words, that male functions will, by progress and development, come into closer resemblance to female functions. Science is wrong, like history, and poetry, and art. But what is science? Just what man knows: — man, who knows nothing; and who is only a grade higher in the scale of being than a chimpanzee! A true science would show you that woman, as a being with no waste organs, no rudimentary powers, stands at the head of all created things.

Milton's Eve — though fairest, wisest, best — is not high enough in the scale for Eliza. Eve is not made first of the twain in Paradise; first, as she ought to be, in virtue of her keener insight, her braver spirit, her larger longings. Nay, the Female Seer grows hot against the Bible for its hard and cruel way of dealing with that story of the Fall; urging that the Scriptures tell the tale as a man was sure to conceive it, to his own advantage, and to woman's loss. She writes it out afresh, and puts the thing in another light.

In this new version of the Fall, Eve is not weak, but strong. She finds Adam in bonds, and she sets him free. He is bound by a bad law to live in a state of darkness and bondage, a mere animal life, without knowing good from evil. She breaks his fetters, and shows him the way to heaven. The consequences of her act are noble; and through her courage Man did not fall, but rise. She did "a great service to humanity," when she plucked the forbidden fruit.

In the details of the Fall, Eliza finds much comfort, when she can read them by her own inward light. Wisdom (in the form of a Serpent) addressed the woman, not the man, who would have cared little for the tree of knowledge. The temptation offered to her was spiritual. She took the forbidden fruit, in the hope of becoming wiser and diviner than she had been. Man followed her. Yes: the ascendancy of woman began in Paradise!

## CHAPTER XX.

### Oneida Creek.

On the opposite verge of thought to the systems of Mother Ann, of Elizabeth Denton, of Eliza Farnham, stands a body of reformers who call themselves, in their dogmatic aspect, Perfectionists, in their social aspect, Bible Communists. These people aver that they have discovered the only way; and have reduced to practice what their rivals in reform have only reduced into talk. They profess to base their theory of family life on the New Testament, most of all on the teachings of St. Paul.

What these Bible People (as they call themselves) have done in the sphere of life and thought has certainly been attempted in no faltering spirit. They have restored, as they say, t'e Divine government of the world; they have put the two sexes on an equal footing; they have declared marriage a fraud and property a theft; they have abolished for themselves all human laws; they have formally renounced their allegiance to the United States.

The founder of this school of reform — a school which boasts already of having its prophets, seminaries, periodicals, and communities — its schism, its revival, its persecutions, its male and female martyrs — is John Humphrey Noyes: a tall, pale man, with sandy hair and beard, grey, dreamy eyes, good mouth, white temples, and a noble forehead. He is a little like Carlyle; and it is the fashion among his people to say that he closely resembles our Chelsea sage; a fiction which is evidently a pleasant delusion to the Saint himself. He has been in turn a graduate of Dartmouth College in New Hampshire, a law clerk at Putney in Vermont, a theological student in Andover, Massachusetts, a preacher at Yale College, New Haven, a seceder from the Congregational Church, an outcast, a heretic, an agitator, a dreamer, an experimentalizer; finally he is now acknowledged by many people as a sect-founder, a revelator, a prophet, enjoying light from heaven and personal intimacies with God.

I have been spending a few days at Oneida Creek, the chief seat of the four societies founded by Noyes — Oneida, Wallingford, New Haven, and New York — as the guest of Father Noyes. I have lived in his family; had a good deal of talk with him; had access to his books and papers, even those of a private nature; had many conversations with the brothers and sisters whom he has gathered into order, both in his presence and apart from him; had leave from him to copy such of the Family papers as I pleased. The account which follows of this extraordinary body of men has been written fresh from their own mouths, and from my own observation, on the spot which it describes.

"You will find," said Horace Greeley, as we parted in New York, "that Oneida communism is a trade success; the rest you will see and judge for yourself."

From Oneida, a young and busy town on the New York Central Railway, a wide and dusty road, on either side of which, behind a line of frame houses and their little gardens, the forest is still green and fresh, leads you to Oneida Creek; a part of that Indian reservation which was left by a compassionate legislature to the Oneidas, one of the Six Nations famous in the early history of New York for their honesty, their good faith, and their constant friendship for the whites. Twenty years ago the Creek ran through a virgin soil. Here and there a loghouse peeped from beneath the trees, in which some remnants of a great and unhappy tribe of hunters stood, as it were, at bay. The water yielded fish, the forest game. The only clearings had been made by fire; woods either burnt by chance or felled for winter fuel. A patch of maize might be seen on some sunny slope; but the Oneida Indian is a very poor farmer at his best; and the district in which he dwelt with his squaw and his papoose, a tangle of briar and swamp and stones, was unbroken to the use of man. He sold his land to a pale-f⁓ ⁓, richer than himself, for a sum of money not ⁓   ⁓ n value to the maple and hickory woods upon it. From this second owner the Perfectionists bought the Creek, with its surrounding woods and open; and in twenty years the surface has been wholly changed. Roads have been cut through the forest; bridges have been built; the Creek has been trained and dammed; mills for slitting planks and for driving wheels have been erected; the bush has been cleared away; a great hall, offices and work-shops have been raised; lawns have been laid out, shrubberies planted, and footways gravelled; orchards and vineyards have been reared and fenced; manufactures have been set going — iron-work, satchel-making, fruit-preserving, silk-spinning; and the whole aspect of this wild forest land has been beautified into the likeness of a rich domain in Kent. Few corners of America can compete in loveliness with the swards and gardens lying about the home of the Oneida family, as these things arrest the eyes of a stranger coming upon them from the rough fields even of the settled region of New York.

The home, which stands on a rising knoll commanding some pretty views, is remarkable without and within; for among the laws which the Bible Communists have put behind them are the seven orders of architecture. The builder of this pile is Erastus Hamilton, once a New York farmer, carpenter, what not, as a New Yorker is apt to be; a man of sense and tact, not much of a scholar, not at all an orator, but a person of some natural gifts, which fit him to be a ruler and contriver in the midst of inferior men. He is the Father of this Oneida family, just as Noyes is the Father of all the Perfectionist families; and being master of the house, so to speak, he is also builder of the house; though he claims that everything in it, from the position of a fire-place to the furnishing of a library, is the result of a special sign from Heaven. I may add, without offence, that Father Hamilton was open to new lights, even when they flashed from a Gentile brain; most of all to those of my fellow-traveller, William Haywood, architect and engineer.

In the centre of the pile, approached by a wide passage and a flight of stairs, is the great hall; a chapel, a theatre, a concert-room, a casino, a working place, all in one; being supplied with benches, lounging-chairs, work-tables, a reading-desk, a stage, a gallery, a pianoforte. In this hall, the sisters play and sew, the elders preach, the librarian (Brother Pitt) reads the news, the young men and maidens make love — so far as such a Gentile art is allowed to live in this curious place. Near the great hall is the drawing-room, properly the ladies' room; and around this chamber stand the sleeping apartments of the family and its guests. Beneath this floor, on either side of the wide passage, are the offices, together with a reception room, a library, a place of business. Kitchen, refectory, fruit-cellar, laundry, are in separate buildings. The store is in front of the home, divided from it by a lawn; and farther away, peeping prettily through the green trees, stand the mills, farms, stables, cowsheds, presses, and general work-shops. The estate is about six hundred acres in extent; the Family gathered under one roof number about three hundred. Everything at Oneida Creek suggests taste, repose, and wealth; and the account-books prove that during the past seven or eight years the Family have been making a good deal of money, which they have usefully laid out, either in the erection of new mills, or in draining and enriching the soil.

The men affect no particular garb; though the loose coat, the wide-awake, and peg-top breeches, common in every part of rural America, make up their ordinary wear. They have no separate dress for Sundays and holidays; having abolished Sundays and holidays along with every other human institution. But they are open to new lights on dress; saying that the last thing has not yet been done in the way of hats and boots. At one of their evening meetings, I heard Brother Pitt, a well-read man, deliver his testimony in favour of peg-tops. The ladies wear a garb which is peculiar, and to my eyes becoming. It may be made of any material and of any colour; though brown and blue for outdoor wear, with white for evening in the meeting-room, are the prevailing tints. Muslin, cotton, and a coarse silk, supply the materials. Ladies have the hair cut short, and parted down the centre. No stays, no crinolines, are worn. A tunic falling to the knee, loose trousers of the same material, a vest buttoning high towards the throat, short hanging sleeves, and a straw hat; these simple articles make up a dress in which a plain woman escapes much notice, and a pretty girl looks winsome. I am told that it is no part of Father Noyes' plan that the young ladies of his family should look bewitching; for such is not his theory of a modest and moral woman's life; but for my own poor self, being only a Gentile and a sinner, I could not help seeing that many of his young disciples have been gifted with rare beauty, and that two of the singing girls, Alice Ackley and Harriet Worden, have a grace and suppleness of form, as well as loveliness of face and hand, to warm a painter's heart.

So much of the Oneida Community you may see in a few hours, if you simply wander about the place, with Brother Bolles, a gentleman who for twenty-five years had been a Methodist preacher in Massachusetts, and who is now a Perfectionist brother in Oneida, with this special duty of receiving ordinary strangers. You see a fine house, a noble lawn, a green shrubbery, orchards shining with apple-trees, pear-trees, plum-trees, cherry-trees, prolific vineyards, excellent farms, busy work-shops, grazing cattle, whizzing mills, and grinding saws — peace, order, beauty, and material wealth; and these are what the pic-nic visitors, who come in thousands to stare and wonder, to hear good music, to eat squash and pastry, always see. They are something; signs of life, but not the life itself. The secrets of this strange success, the foundations on which this community rests, the social features which sustain it, are of deeper interest than the fact itself: and these mysteries of the Society are not explained to pic-nic parties by Brother Bolles.

It is well known that all the Communistic trials which have been made in England, Germany, and America, from Rapp's Harmony, and Owen's New Harmony, down to Cabet's Icaria, have been failures. Men with brains, women with hearts, have often turned from what they deem the evils of competition to what they hope may prove the saving principles of association; but no body of such reformers, with the sole exception of your wifeless followers of Ann

Lee, have ever yet been able to work an association in which they held a community of goods. Each failure may have had its own history, its own explanation, showing how near it came to success; but the fact of failure cannot be denied. The Socialists had to quit New Lanark; the Rappists had to sell Harmony; the Icarians have been swept from Nauvoo. Liberty, equality, fraternity, have not hitherto paid their weekly bills; and a society that does not pay its expenses, must, in the long run, go to the wall, even though it should, in other respects, reproduce the image of paradise on the earth. Man may not sit all day under a palm-tree, munching his creel of dates, and feeling at peace with heaven and earth. Want prods him forward; and he has no choice but one of the two evils — either to work or die. Each trial and failure of association puts the principle into peril. See what you come to, laughs the Sadducee, happy in his broad lands, his mansions, gardens, vineyards, when you disturb the order of time, of nature, and of Providence! You come to waste, to beggary, and death. Competition, which is the soul of trade, for ever, and blessed be heaven, which fights on the side of the great capitalists!

If the theory of mutual help, as against that of self-help, be the true principle of social life, as so many men say, so many women feel, why have nearly all the attempts to live by it, and under it, ended in disaster?

"I tell you," said Father Noyes to me this morning, "they have all failed because they were not founded on Bible truth. Religion is at the root of life; and a safe social theory must always express a religious truth. Now there are four stages in the true organisation of a family; (1) Reconciliation with God; (2) Salvation from sin; (3) Brotherhood of man and woman; (4) Community of labour and of its fruits. Owen, Ripley, Fourier, Cabet, began at the third and fourth stages; they left God out of their tale, and they came to nothing."

Noyes makes no secret of his opinion that he has contrived, by the Divine favour, a new and perfect system of society; that he has already established by trial the chief principles of the new domestic order; and that it only remains for the communities of Oneida, Wallingford, and Brooklyn, to work out a few details, in order to its universal adoption in the United States. If the reader cares to hear how this man — who has done so much in America, and of whom so little is known in England — came to think as he does on the religious aspects and bearings of domestic life — I will put before him, as openly as a layman dare, the results of my enquiries at Oneida Creek.

## CHAPTER XXI.

#### Holiness.

WHILE he was yet living at Putney, in Vermont, as a lawyer's clerk, Noyes was struck by that fierce revival of '31, which wrecked so many New England barques. Noyes is said to have suddenly grown grave and moody; all his lights appear to have gone out, leaving him in the dark night, amidst howling storms, against which his puny strength of intellect could make no head. Turning his gaze inwards, he became, as he told me, conscious of sin and death. How could he free himself from these evils? Feeling the world and the devil strong within him, he abandoned law, taking up with the older science of theology. While studying in his new course at Andover, he fell into many temptations, ate and drank freely, and gave way to many other seductions of the flesh. The young divines, his fellow-students in the college, were a bad set, who laughed at revival energies, and sneered at the religious world. Noyes thought he would go away from Andover; seeking the Lord elsewhere, and on opening the Bible, his eye fell upon the conclusive text, "He is not here!" With this warning from Heaven before his eyes, he went away from Andover to Yale College, at New Haven, where he became a great seeker after truth, — not of the truth as it stands between God and man only, but of the truth as between man and man. In the midst of dreams as wild (I infer) as ever visited the brain of an Arab, there was always about Noyes a practical American view of things. He felt that the Divine plan must be perfect; that if he could read that plan, he would find in it an Order of the Earth, no less than an Order of Heaven. What is that Order of the Earth? Not the Pagan law under which we live. He turned for light to the written word. In the Bible, he says, he sought for that rule of life which the schools could not teach him. Pondering the words of the gospel, and conning by himself the writings of Paul, he found in these original documents of the Church a comfort which the preachers of New Haven had not proved to his soul that they held in gift. Paul spoke to his heart; but in a sense, as he asserts, quite foreign to that in which the apostle had been understood at Antioch and Rome.

Much reading of Paul's epistles led him to believe that the Christian faith, as it appears in the Churches of Europe and America, even in those which style themselves reformed, is a huge historical mistake. There is no visible Church of Christ on earth. The Church of Paul and Peter was the true one; a community of brothers, of equals, of saints; but it passed away at an early date, our Lord having returned in the Spirit, as He had promised, to dwell among His people evermore. On this second advent, Noyes says that our Lord abolished the old law; closing the empire of Adam, cleansing His children from their sin, and setting up His kingdom in the hearts of all who would accept His reign. Noyes fixes this spiritual advent in the year 70, immediately after the fall of Jerusalem; since which date, he says, there have been one true Church, and many false churches, bearing His name; — a Church of His saints, men sinless in body and in soul; confessing Him as their prince; taking upon them a charge of holiness; rejecting law and usage, and submitting their passions to His will; and, churches of the world, built up in man's art and pride, with thrones and societies, prelates and cardinals, and popes; churches of the screw, the faggot and the rack, having their forms and oaths, their hatreds and divisions, their anathemas, celibacies, and excommunications. The devil, says Noyes, began his reign on the very same day with Christ, and the official churches of Greece and Rome, together with their half-reformed brethren in England and America, are the capital provinces of the devil's empire. The kingdoms of the earth are Satan's: yet the Perfect Society, founded by Paul, into which Christ descended as a living spirit, never quite perished from out of men's hearts, but, by the grace of God, kept an abiding witness for itself, until the time should come for reviving the apostolic faith and practice, not in a corrupted Europe, a worn-out Asia, but in the fresh and green communities of the United States. Some high and vestal natures kept the flame alive. The day for this true Church came. Faith, banished from the busy crowd, returned to the young seekers after truth at Yale; and the family of Christ, after being corrupted in Antioch, persecuted in Rome, and caricatured in London, is now refounded at Wallingford, Brooklyn, and Oneida Creek!

In this new American sect, — a church as well as a school, — the rule of faith and the rule of life are equally plain. The Perfectionist has a right to do what he likes. Of course he will tell you (as my host at Oneida tells me) that from the nature of the case he can do nothing but what is good. The Holy Spirit sustains and guards him. Some may go wrong through the old Adam being fierce within them; but a few exceptions do not kill an eternal truth. We hold that a king can do no wrong, though a good deal of scandal, tempered by daggers and actresses, may afflict our royal and imperial courts. A Perfectionist knows no law; neither that pronounced from Sinai, and repeated from Gerizim, nor that which is administered in Washington and New York. He does not live under law, but under God: that is to say, under what his own mind prompts him to do, as being right. The Lord has made him free. To him, the word is nothing: its force having been wholly spent for him at the Second Coming. No commandment in the Ten, no statute on the rolls, is binding upon him, — a child of grace, delivered from the power of the law, and from the stain of sin. Laws are for sinners — he is a saint; other men fall into temptation — he is sealed and reclaimed by the Holy Ghost.

This frame of mind, which is not unlikely to look like rebellion in the eyes of a Gentile, is called by the Bible Communists, a state of submission. In this world you can only choose whom you will serve. You cannot have two masters, — God and Mammon. Earth is not perfect; Christ is Perfect. In confessing Christ, you give up the world, yielding it bodily, thoroughly, and for ever. No half-measure will suffice to save you; and the whole tendency of American thought (before the War) being in favour of individuals as against institutions, no one felt much surprise on hearing that Noyes and his adherents had made a formal renunciation of their duty to the United States. Others had done the same thing before him; Shakers, Tunkers, Mormons, Socialists, Icarians, and many more. In fact, not a few Americans of the higher class had come to regard the State as a kind of political club, from which they might withdraw at pleasure; but the Perfectionist went far beyond the Socialist, the Shaker, and the Mormon, in his renunciation, for he rejected the law of God as well as the laws of men; the civil code, the statutes at large, the canons, and decrees, the Ten Commandments, the Lord's Prayer, the Sermon on the Mount; all his old voluntary and involuntary rules, from his temperance pledge to his marriage vows. Nothing of the old man, the old citizen, was left to him. He denied the churches, he renounced his obligations, he defied the magistrates and the police. In his obedience to God, he cast away all the safeguards invented by man. Noyes had been a teetotaller; on assuming holiness, he began to drink ardent spirits. He had been temperate as a Brahman; he now indulged his palate with highly-spiced meats. He had been chaste in his habits, regular in his hours of sleep; he now began to stay out all night, to wander about the quays, to lie in door-ways, to visit infamous houses, to consort with courtesans and thieves. In defending himself against men who cannot reconcile such a mode of living with the profession of holiness, Noyes asserts that he had given himself up to temptation, but the power in which he trusted for protection had been strong enough to save him. He had drunk, and gorged, and wantoned with the flesh, in order to escape from the bonds of system. As he puts the matter to himself, he said, "Can I trust God for morality? Can I trust my passions, desires, propensities, everything within me which has hitherto been governed by worldly rules and my own volition, to the paramount mercy of God's Spirit?" He answered to himself that he could and would put his faith, his conduct, his salvation, in the keeping of the Holy Ghost; and in this confidence, he says, he walked through the house of sin untouched, as the Hebrew children stood unscathed in the midst of fire.

But how, it may be asked, does a man arrive at this stage of grace? Nothing (if I understand it) is more easy. You have only to wish it, and the thing is done. Good works are not necessary, prayers are not desirable; nothing serves a man but faith. You stand up in public, by the side of some brother in the Lord, and take upon yourself a profession of Christ. You say, you are freed from the power of sin, and the stain is suddenly washed from your soul. In this American creed, facts would appear to lie in wait for words, and all that is said is apparently also done. "He stood up and confessed Holiness," — such is the form of announcing that a lamb has been brought into the fold of Father Noyes.

When Noyes began to preach his doctrine, some years ago, the spirit of separation was alive and active in every part of New England; and many persons thought that the only hope of staying this impetus of the American mind towards social chaos lay in the principle of association then being tested in such experiments as Mount Lebanon, New Harmony, and Brook Farm. In such a state of confusion, it is no marvel that Noyes should have failed to see that his theory of Individual Action, as he first conceived it, could not work. A man may be a law to himself; but how can he be a law to another man, who is also bound to be a law to himself? Noyes may receive from his own conscience a guiding light; and Hamilton may receive from his own conscience a guiding light: each may be sufficient for its purpose; but how can Noyes' light become a rule for Hamilton, Hamilton's for Noyes, unless by a bargain between the two? If they could not make such a bargain, they must dwell apart; if they could compromise the affair as to these two lights, they came under law. From this alternative they have no escape: on one side chaos, on the other law.

Noyes found himself in trouble the day he began to live with his male and female disciples according to their notions of celestial order — not under law, but under grace; and before the community could exist as a fact, a second principle had to be introduced.

This second principle is called Sympathy; and the office which it holds in the Family is very much like that which the world assigns to Public Opinion. Sympathy corrects the individual will, and reconciles nature with obedience, liberty with light.

Thus, a brother may do anything he likes; but he is trained to do everything in sympathy with the general wish. If the public judgment is against him, he is wrong — that is to say, he is going away from the path of grace; and his only chance of happiness lies in going back to what is most agreeable to the common mind. The Family is supposed to be always wiser than the unit.

A man who wants anything for himself — say, a new hat, a holiday, a young damsel's smiles — must consult with one of the Elders and see how the brotherhood feels on the subject of his wish. If their sympathy is not with him, he retires from his suit. When the matter is of moment, he seeks the advice of a committee of Elders, who may choose to refer it to the Family in their evening sittings.

It was long before this second great principle was introduced as a ruling power, and until it was introduced, the community of Perfect Saints had little of what the world would call success.

## CHAPTER XXII.

#### A Bible Family.

WHILE Noyes was still a preacher of Holiness, going about among the churches, he made converts of Abigail Merwin (a woman was necessary to him, and Abigail was a female disciple of whom he might feel proud) and James Boyle; and these two early followers were the first apostates from his creed. Abigail seems to have expected an offer of marriage; Boyle had hopes of being elected pope; but neither of these pretensions suited Father Noyes, who felt averse to wedlock, and meant to be pope himself. They were only the first seceders; for as time wore on, and the true principle of Holiness was understood among his people, the units fell away from the mass. Each man was a law to himself; the spirit operated in single minds; and out of many independent members it was impossible to found a church. No one would concede, no one obey, no one unite. At the end of four years' labour, Noyes stood alone; all his beloved disciples having gone their way; some into the world, others into heresies, many into older sects, from which they had been drawn by him. The press had opened fire upon them. Noyes had been denounced as crazy; a charge to which his conduct and preaching oftentimes exposed him. There were still Perfectionists, but Noyes was not their pope.

Taught by painful trials that ropes cannot be spun out of sand, he turned, as so many others were at that time turning, to the principle of association — with him it must be Bible Association — for a future. Cast adrift from his old friends of New Haven, he went back to his father's house at Putney, in Vermont, where he had been first awakened into spiritual life, and there he began his work of converting the world afresh, by founding a Bible class, and teaching a few simple and rustic persons the way of grace. Some listened to his words; for never, perhaps, since the days of Herod the Great, certainly not since the years preceding the English Civil War, had any people ever found itself in a moral chaos so strange as that which prevailed in the United States. Abigail Merwin had declared on quitting the sect, that their gospel freedom ran into indecency. The same thing had been said in the streets of Jerusalem and in the streets of London; but while the Gentiles of New York laughed at these stories, the believers waxed in zeal. What were the world and its ways to them? The Putney class grew strong in purpose, if not in numbers; for Noyes having come to see that quality of converts, rather than quantity, was of moment to him, now bent the force of his genius, which was great and original, upon the dozen hearers whom his voice had called together in this native town; until he could transform the Bible class into a Bible Family; in other words, until he had made them ready in soul and body for the great experiment of dwelling in one house, free from the trammels, everywhere else endured, of living under law.

To lodge a family of converts under one roof, the teacher required a large house. A large house, even in Vermont, where the dwellings are built of wood, costs money, and Father Noyes was poor. His life had been that of a wanderer to and fro; resting-place he had none; and the shepherd, like his sheep, was without shelter from the storm. Among his disciples in Vermont, there was a young lady named Harriet Holton, a girl of good family, with present means and some expectations. Such a young lady would be a blessing to him in every way, if he could only obtain her as a wife; but then his principles stood in the way. Marriage being utterly against his doctrine of the true gospel life, how was he to get her person and her money into his power? Of course, he could not offer his hand and his heart in the usual way, since she had heard him declaim against wedlock as the sign of a degenerate state. In fact, if he proposed to her at all — and his need for her dollars was very sore — he would be compelled to say that he should not expect her to be true to him only, and that he would certainly not engage to be true to her. But Harriet's position was out of the common way. She had no father, no mother, no brother, no sister. Her only kinsman was an aged and foolish grandfather. She had been in love with a young man who wished to marry her, but the old man had interfered to prevent him; on which the girl had fallen sick, and in a fit of remorse her grandfather had sworn an oath that in future she should do as she pleased, and he would willingly abide her wishes. Thus, a way had been opened, as it were, for Noyes to come in with his proposal, which conveyed to her an offer of his hand in the following words (a copy of which has been given to me by himself): —

## A LOVE LETTER.

*Father Noyes to Harriet A. Holton.*

*Putney, June 11, 1838.*

BELOVED SISTER, — After a deliberation of more than a year, in patient waiting, and watching for indications of the Lord's will, I am now permitted — and indeed happily constrained — by a combination of favourable circumstances to propose to you a partnership which I will not call marriage, till I have defined it.

As believers, we are already one with each other, and with all saints. This primary and universal union is more radical, and of course more important than any partial and external partnership; and with reference to this, it is said, "there is neither male or female," neither marrying nor giving in marriage in heaven. With this in view, we can enter into no engagements with each other, which shall limit the range of our affections, as they are limited in matrimonial engagements, by the fashion of this world. I desire and expect my yoke-fellow will love all who love God, whether they be male or female, with a warmth and strength of affection unknown to earthly lovers, and as freely as if she stood in no particular connexion with me. In fact, the object of my connexion with her will be, not to monopolize and enslave her heart or my own, but to enlarge and establish both in the free fellowship of God's universal family. If the external union and companionship of a man and woman in accordance with these principles is properly called marriage, I know that marriage exists in heaven, and I have no scruple in offering you my heart and hand, with an engagement to be married in due form, as soon as God shall permit.

At first I designed to set before you *many* weighty reasons for this proposal; but upon second thought, I prefer the attitude of a witness to that of an advocate, and shall therefore only suggest, briefly, a few matter-of-fact considerations, leaving the advocacy of the case to God — the customary persuasions and romance to your own imagination — and more particular explanations to a personal interview.

1. In the plain speech of a witness, not of a flatterer, I respect and love you for many desirable qualities, spiritual, intellectual, moral, and personal; and especially for your faith, kindness, simplicity, and modesty.

2. I am confident that the partnership I propose will greatly promote our mutual happiness and improvement.

3. It will also set us free, at least myself, from

much reproach, and many evil surmisings, which are occasioned by celibacy in present circumstances.

4. It will enlarge our sphere and increase our means of usefulness to the people of God.

5. I am willing at this particular time, to testify by example, that I am a follower of Paul, in holding that "marriage is honourable in all."

6. I am also willing to testify practically against that "bondage of liberty" which utterly sets at naught the ordinances of men, and refuses to submit to them even for the Lord's sake. I know that the immortal union of hearts — everlasting honey-moon, which alone is worthy to be called marriage, can never be *made* by a ceremony, and I know equally well that such a marriage can never be *marred* by a ceremony. You are aware that I have no profession save that of a servant of God — a profession which has thus far subjected me to many vicissitudes, and has given me but little of this world's prosperity. If you judge me by the outward appearance, or the future by the past, you will naturally find, in the irregularity and seeming instability of my character and fortune, many objections to a partnership. Of this I will only say, that I am conscious of possessing, by the grace of God, a spirit of firmness, perseverance, and faithfulness in every good work, which has made the vagabond, incoherent service, to which I have thus far been called, almost intolerable to me; and I shall welcome heaven's order for my release from it as an exile after seven years' pilgrimage would welcome the sight of his home. I see now no reason why I should not have a "cer-

tain dwelling-place," and enter upon a course which is consistent with the duties of domestic life. Perhaps your reply to this will be the voice saying to me, —

> "Watchman! let thy wanderings cease,
> Hie thee to thy quiet home."

Yours in the Lord,
J. H. Noyes.

Harriet, left to herself, answered as the preacher wished; in a few days they were united; and Noyes expended her seven thousand dollars in building a house and a printing-office, in buying presses and types, and in starting a newspaper. So long as the old man lived, he supplied them with money to live on; when he died Father Noyes came in for nine thousand dollars in one lump. He makes no secret of the fact that he married Harriet for her money; to use his own words, she was given to him as his reward for preaching the Truth.

The first family gathered into celestial order at Putney included the Preacher's wife, his mother, his sister, and his brother; all of whom have remained true to his theory of domestic life. His mother died only a few days before my arrival at Oneida Creek; an aged lady, who went to her rest (I am told) confident that the system introduced by her son is the only true and perfect society of Christian men and women on the earth.

These persons, with a few preachers, farmers, doctors, and their wives and daughters, all men of means, character, and position, went to live in the same house; setting up, as they oddly phrased it, a branch of the heavenly business in Putney, after a formal renunciation of the Republican Government, and an everlasting secession from the United States.

And now began for them a new life, more daring, more original than that which Ripley, Dana, and Hawthorn, tried to follow at Brook Farm. They stopped all prayer and religious service, they put down Sunday, they broke up family ties, and without separating anybody, put an end to the selfish relations of husband and wife. All property was thrown into a common stock; all debts, all duties, fell upon the Society, which ate in one room, slept under one roof, and lived upon one store. At first they were strict and stern with each other; for written codes being all set aside, as things of the old world, they had no means of guiding weak, of controlling wicked brethren save that of free Criticism on their conduct; a system of government which had yet to become a saving power. The life was somewhat hard. Three hours were spent each morning in the hall; one hour in studying such books of history as might help them to understand the Bible better; one hour either in silence or in reading the Scriptures; a third hour in discussing the things which they had read and thought. Mid-day was given to labour on the farm; evening to study, reading, music, and society. One person gave lessons to the rest in either Greek or Hebrew; a second read aloud some English or German writer on hermeneutics; and a third stood up and criticised his brother saint. In the midst of these incessant labours, the old Adam

13*

appeared amongst them, and slew their peace. One man ate too much, a second drank too much, a third ran wild in love. Strife arose among the brethren, leading in turn to gossip among their neighbours, to queries about them in the local press, to attacks in the surrounding grog-shops, and at length into suits in the Gentile courts. What they had most to fear in their little Eden was gospel freedom in the matter of goods and wives.

Noyes admits that the Devil found a way into the second Eden as into the first; and that in Putney, as in Paradise, the Evil One worked his evil will through woman. When the moral disorder in his little paradise could be no longer hidden, he became very angry and very sad. How was he to bear this cross? A sudden change from legal restraints to gospel liberties, must needs be a trial to the lusts of man. But how could he make distinctions in the work of God? God had given to man his passions, appetites and powers. These powers and appetites are free. Desire has its use and faculty in the heavenly system; and when the soul is free, all use implies the peril of abuse. Must, then, the Saints come under bonds? He could not see it. Aware that many of his people had disgraced the profession of Holiness, he still said to himself, in the words of St. Paul, "Must I go back because offences come?" To go back was for him to tear up his Bible and lay down his work. Such a return was beyond his desire, and beyond his power: so he laboured on with his people, curbing the unruly, guiding the careless, and expelling the impenitent. As he put the case to himself: — If a man were moving from one town to another, he could not hope to do it without moil and dirt, how then could he expect to change his place of toil from earth to heaven without suffering damage by the way? Waste is incident to change. His people were unprepared for so sharp a trial; and the quarrels which had come upon them, scandalising Windham County, and scattering many of the Saints, were laid by him to the account of those who were as yet unused to the art of living under grace.

Some rays of comfort fell upon Noyes in this hour of his failure and distress. A rival body of Perfectionists, of which Mahan was pope, and Taylor prime minister, had set up an Eden of their own at Oberlin, in Lorain County, Ohio. Mahan pretended to see visions, to converse with angels, and to receive communications direct from God. Taylor, an able editor and eloquent preacher, made also some pretensions to celestial gifts. Now, between Noyes and Mahan, Putney and Oberlin, there had reigned a fraternal feud, like that which disgraced the two sons of Eve. According to all the Perfectionist prophets, Holiness and Liberty are the two primary elements in the atmosphere of heaven, — that is to say, of a perfect society; but in the exercise of their daily right of following, each man his own lights, these prophets had come to regard the two elements as of unequal value; so that strife arose between them, questions were debated, and schools were formed. One party, putting freedom before holiness, were known as the "Liberty men;" another, putting sanctity before freedom, were known as the "Holiness men." Putney stood out for holiness; Oberlin for liberty; though both affected to renounce the world, and to admit no tutelage but that of God. Noyes attacked Oberlin in the 'Witness;' Taylor answered in the 'Evangelist;' and the war of words went raging on for years, until Putney fell away into quarrels; and Taylor had used his freedom in a fashion to provoke the interference of a Gentile court.

## CHAPTER XXIII.

### New Foundations.

WHEN Putney had become too warm a place for Noyes and his Bible Family to live in; not, as he told me, on account of any persecution from the churches of religious Vermont, but solely from the opposition of drunken and worthless rowdies; the Preacher, having let his house and farm to a Gentile, moved away from his native town to Oneida Creek; a place which, on account of its beauty, its remoteness, and its fertility, seemed favourable to his plan of trying, by patient industry, to lay a new foundation for social and family life. Mary Cragin, who brought with her George, her husband, and some other friends already tried in the fire, came heartily into his scheme; becoming to this fresh enterprise, all that Margaret Fuller would have liked to be, and was not, in the less daring settlement of Brook Farm.

About fifty men, with as many women, and nearly as many children, put their means together, built a frame-house and offices, bought a patch of land, which they began to clear and stock; and once more giving up the world, its usages, its rights, declared their Family separated from the United States, from the society of men, even as Abraham and his seed had been separated from the people of the

Hauran. The new Bible Family announced itself as a branch of the visible kingdom of heaven. Many of the Saints having been at Putney, they had some experience in the ways of grace; and Noyes laid down for them a rule in their new home, which a Gentile would have thought superfluous at Oneida Creek, — the duty of enjoying life. At Putney, said he, they had been too strict; studying overmuch; dealing too harshly with each other's faults. In their new home, heaven would not ask from them such rigours. If God, he asked them, had meant Adam to fast and pray, would he have placed him in a garden tempted on every side by delicious fruit? No; man's Maker had blessed him with appetites, and then turned him into a clover-field! And what were these saints at Oneida Creek? Men in the position of Adam before the fall; men without sin; men to whom everything was lawful because everything was pure. Why, then, should they not eat, drink, and love, to their heart's content, under daily guidance of the Holy Spirit?

They made no rules, they chose no chiefs. Every man was to be a rule to himself, every woman to herself; and as to rulers, they declared that nature and education make men masters of their fellows, putting them in the places which they are born and trained to fill; another way of saying that God was to rule in person, with Father Noyes for his visible pope and king. All property was made over to Christ; and the use of it only was reserved for those who had united themselves to Him. The wives and children of the Family were to be as common as the loaves and fishes; the very soul of the new society being a mystery very difficult to explain in English phrase.

Through a dozen years of sharp and feverish trial the society held its ground. War without, and want within, exposed the brethren to temptations, which no body of zealots but a band of New England farmers, artisans, and professional men, could have lived through. Mary Cragin was drowned in the Hudson river, and it was long before a woman could be found to take her place. Noyes made overtures to Abigail Mervin, his first disciple, whom he still professed to love in the spirit. Abigail would not listen. She is still alive, I may add, and Noyes still dreams of drawing her back into his fold. Sister Skinner became the female leader — Mother of the Family; but she is now living at Wallingford; and Sister Dunn is nominal Mother at Oneida Creek. Her hold of office seems to me but weak; and I think that either Sister Joslyn, a poetess, or Sister Helen Noyes, may now be considered the presiding goddess of Oneida Creek. But as power is only held by sympathy, the spells of these ladies may be shared by the two singers, Sister Alice and Sister Harriet. I speak as one who has lived under the charm. In spite of their rude fare and their hard life, strange people came and joined them; a Massachusetts preacher, a Canadian trapper, a reader for the London press. Of all these converts to the kingdom of heaven, he who might have been counted as the man least likely to be useful to such a colony, the Canadian trapper, proved in the end to be the actual founder of their fortunes. As yet, the Saints had given themselves heart and soul to the land, like those Shakers, from whom Noyes (as Elder Frederick told me) had learnt his first lesson in social economy; but the arts of growing apples, potting pears, and making syrups, are too common in America for any body to think of gaining a fortune by them. The Family did its best; its best was very good. Last year, as I saw by their books, they sold twenty-five thousand dollars' worth of preserved fruits. But the lawns and gardens, the stately home, and the busy mills of Oneida, were not made out of apple-trees and peach trees. They came, in the main part, from the cunning hands of Sewell Newhouse, this Canadian trapper.

One of the great trades of America is that of traps. Traps are wanted of many kinds, for the land is covered with vermin, from the huge bear of the Rocky Mountains down to the common field mouse; but the Yankee mechanic, so prolific in the matter of cork-screws, sewing-frames, and nut-crackers has left the manufacture of traps to Solingen and Elberfeld, so that western and northern America have been hitherto supplied with traps from beyond the Rhine. Now Brother Newhouse, when he settled down to machine work at Oneida Creek, saw, as an old trapper, that the German article, though good and even cheap in its way, might be much improved; and taking the thing in hand, he soon made it lighter in weight, simpler in form, more deadly in spring. The Oneida Trap became the talk of Madison County and of the State of New York. Orders for it poured in; mechanics were employed, forges were built; and in a few months the German article was a saleless drug in the New York stores. In a single year the Family made eighty thousand dollars of profit by their traps; and although the income has fallen off since others have begun to imitate this product of the Saints, the revenue derived from the sale of Oneida traps is still about three thousand pounds English money in the year.

At first thought, there seems to be something comic in the fact of a kingdom of heaven being dependent for its daily bread on the sale of traps. As I walked through the forges with Father Hamilton, I could not help saying that such work seemed rather strange for a colony of Saints. He answered, with a very grave face, that the Earth is lying under a curse, that vermin are a consequence of that curse, that the Saints have to make war upon them and destroy them — whence the perfect legitimacy of their trade in traps! It is not in the State of New York, where every man is a pleader and a casuist, that any one is found at a loss for arguments in favour of that which brings grist to his mill.

Anyhow, they made the traps, and then the traps made them.

What may be called the home affairs of the Family seem to have been keeping pace with their outward and commercial progress. The theory of ruling the more disorderly spirits by means of sympathy, was raised from an idea into a 'science; and the chief business of the evening meetings has now become the evolution of this sympathy as a ruling power by means of free criticism. I was present at one of these meetings, when Sydney Joslyn, a son of the poetess of Oneida Creek, was subjected to a searching public enquiry. Brother Pitt led the way, describing the young man, mentally and morally; pointing out, with seeming kindliness, but also with astonishing frankness, all the evil things he had ever seen in Sydney — his laziness, his sensuality, his love of dress and show, his sauciness of speech, his lack of reverence. Father Noyes, Father Hamilton, and Brother Bolles followed Pitt, with observations almost equally severe; then came Sister Joslyn, the culprit's mother, who certainly did not spare the rod; and after her rose up Mother Dunn, and a cloud of witnesses. Most of these persons spoke of his good deeds, and two or three hinted that, with all his faults Sydney was a man of genius, a true saint, a credit to Oneida; but the balance of testimony was decidedly against the prisoner on his trial. No man is allowed to reply in person and on the spot. A friend may put in a good word, so as to modify harsh and unfair judgments; but the person under censure must retire from the ordeal to his chamber, sleep on the catalogue of his virtues, so abundantly filled up by his associates; and if he has anything to say either in acceptance or in refusal of the heavy charges made against him by word of mouth, he must put that answer into writing, addressed to the whole community in their meeting-room, not to any individual traducer by name.

On the evening after this testimony had been heard against Sydney Joslyn, the following letter in reply was read in the great hall: —

To the Community.

I take this occasion to express my thanks for the criticism and advice I received last evening, and for the sincerity that was manifested.

I wish to thank Mr. Noyes for his sincerity, especially in regard to times long past. I well remember when I felt very near him and used to converse freely with him; and I consider those my happiest days. I have always regretted my leaving him as I did. I *loved* him, and I am sure that had I continued with him, I should have been a better man and a greater help to him and the Community. I am certain that my love for him *then* has helped me a great deal *since* and has been steadily growing ever since, in spite of adverse circumstances, and in my darkest hours his spirit shone forth and strengthened me and helped to dispel evil spirits. I wish to confess my love for Mr. Hamilton and my confidence in him as a leader. I thank him sincerely for his long-continued patience with me and his untiring efforts to bring me near to Christ and the Community.

I confess Christ the controller of my tongue and a spirit of humility.     Sydney.

What, however, struck me most about these criticisms, next to their obvious use in the art of governing men who have set aside human laws, was not so much their candour as their subtlety. Many of the observations were extremely delicate and deep, showing fine powers of analysis, sharpened by daily practice.

I should not omit to say, that although many young men bore witness against Sydney, no young woman had anything to say about him. The elder ladies were free enough, and one ancient dame exhibited a frankness which would have been hard for a Gentile youth to bear in silence. The reason of this was, not that the girls all liked him, and refrained from criticism, but that, as girls and young women, they could have had little to do with him, and could therefore have told none of his faults. But here we are touching on one of the deepest of the many mysteries of Oneida Creek.

The Family has neither practising lawyer nor doctor in its ranks; on the other hand, it affects to have no quarrels, and to enjoy perfect health. Following the old rule of America — a rule derived from provincial England — the Family breaks its fast at six in the morning, dines at twelve, sups at six in the evening; very much as the Arabs, and the children of nature everywhere, eat and drink at sunrise, noon, and sunset. A few of the weaker saints eat flesh of bird and beast; the more advanced eat only herbs and fruit. Father Noyes eats flesh from habit, but very little of it, having proved by trial that it is not necessary for his health. A party of the Saints went up into Canada last fall, under Newhouse, to trap beaver; they had five weeks of very hard life, and came back from the forests strong and well. None of the Family drink wine and beer, unless it be a dose of either cherry-wine, or gooseberry-wine, taken as a cordial. I tasted three or four kinds of this home-made wine, and agree with Father Noyes that his people will be better without such drinks.

## CHAPTER XXIV.

#### Pantagamy.

How shall I describe, in English words, the innermost social life so freely opened to my view by these religious zealots of Oneida Creek? To an Arab family I could easily shape the matter, so as to leave out nothing of importance to my tale, for the Arabs have derived from their fathers a habit of calling things by the simplest names. We English have another mood; that of hushing up nature in a fine sense of silence; of spending our curiosity on facts about trees, birds, fishes, insects; while we are carefully putting under dark covers anything that relates to the life and nature of man.

George Cragin, one of Mary Cragin's sons, a young man of parts and culture, above all, of erect moral feeling, fresh from college, where he has taken his medical degree, told me in one of our morning rambles, as he might have told a brother whom he loved, the whole history of his heart — the first budding of his affections — the way in which his love was treated — his sense of shame — his passionate desires — his training in the arts of self-restraint and self-control (which is the discipline of his life as a religious man), from the moment of adolescence down to the very hour in which we talked together at Oneida Creek. That little history of one human soul, in its secret strivings, is the strangest story I have ever either heard or read. I wrote it down from the young man's lips, as we sat under the apple-trees — that tale of all he had ever felt, and learned, and suffered, in the school of love; told, as he told it, with a grave face, a modest manner, and in a scientific spirit; but I have no right to print one line of the confession which lies before me now. I saw at Oneida Creek a hundred records of a similar kind, though most of them were less complete in detail and in plan. Some day, in the coming years, such records may be gained for science, and become the bases, perhaps, of new theories in physiology and economics. At present they are sealed, and must be sealed. "They are laid up," said Brother Bolles, "these histories of emotion, until society is ready to receive and use them; when philosophers begin to study the life of man as they now study that of bees, we Bible Communists shall be able to supply them with a multitude of cases carefully observed."

The very core of their domestic system is a relation of the sexes to each other, which they call "a complex marriage." A community of goods, they say, implies a community of wives. Father Noyes maintains that it is a blunder to say either that a man can only love once in his life, or that he can only love one object at one time. "Men and women," he says, "find universally that their susceptibility to love is not burnt out by one honeymoon, or satisfied by one lover. On the contrary, the secret history of the human heart will bear out the assertion that it is capable of loving any number of times, and any number of persons; and that the more it loves, the more it can love. This is the law of nature." Hence, in the Bible Family living at Oneida Creek, the central domestic fact of the household is the complex marriage of its members to each other, and to all; a rite which is to be understood as taking place on the entrance of every new member, whether male or female, into association; and which is said to convert the whole body into one marriage circle; every man becoming the husband and brother of every woman; every woman the wife and sister of every man. Marriage itself, as a rite and as a fact, they have abolished for ever, in the name of true religion; declaring their belief that so selfish and exclusive an institution will be spurned by all honest churches the very next moment after the world is rid of the false idea that love is an act of sin.

That I may not be suspected of colouring by a word or tint the actual practice of this strange fraternity, I will give the statement of his social theory, drawn up for me by Father Noyes himself: —

### Father Noyes on Love.

"The Communities believe, contrary to the theory of sentimental novelists and others, that the affections can be controlled and guided, and that they will produce far better results when rightly controlled and rightly guided, than if left to take care of themselves without any restraint or guidance. They entirely reject the idea, that love is an inevitable fatality which must have its own course. They believe the whole matter of love and its expression should be subject to enlightened self-control, and should be managed for the greatest good. In the Communities it is under the special supervision of the fathers and mothers: in other words, of the wisest and best members, and is often under discussion in the evening meetings, and is also subordinate to the institution of criticism. The fathers and mothers are guided in their management by certain general principles, which have been worked out and are well understood in the Communities. One is termed the principle of the ascending fellowship. It is regarded as better for the young of both sexes to associate in love with persons older than themselves, and, if possible, with those who are spiritual, and have been some time in the school of self-control. This is only another form of the popular principle of contrast. It is well understood by physiologists that it is undesirable for persons of similar characters and temperaments to mate together. Communists have discovered that it is not desirable for two inexperienced and unspiritual persons to rush into fellowship with each other: that it is far better for both to associate with persons of mature character and sound sense.

"Another general principle, well understood in the Communities, is, that it is not desirable for two persons to become exclusively attached to each other — to worship and idolize each other — however popular this experience may be with sentimental people generally. They regard exclusive idolatrous attachment as unhealthy and pernicious, wherever it may exist. The Communists insist that the heart should be kept free to love all the true and worthy, and should never be contracted with exclusiveness, or idolatry, or purely selfish love in any form.

"Another principle well known, and carried out in the Community, is, that no person shall be obliged to receive, at any time, or under any circumstances, the attention of those whom they do not like. The Communities are pledged to protect all their members from disagreeable social approaches. Every woman is free to refuse every man's attentions.

"Still another principle is, that it is best for men in their approaches to women to invite personal interviews through the intervention of a third party, for two important reasons, viz.: first, that the matter may be brought, in some measure, under the inspection of the Community, and secondly, that the women may decline proposals, if they choose, without embarrassment or restraint.

"Under the operation of these general principles, but little difficulty attends the practical carrying out of the social theory of the Communities. As fast as the members become enlightened, they govern themselves by these very principles. The great aim is to teach every one self-control. This leads to the greatest happiness in love and the greatest good to all......"

The style of living at Oneida Creek gives a good deal of power to women, much beyond what they enjoy under law; and this increase of power is a capital point in every new system of social order in the States. Something of this increased power of the female at Oneida Creek I have seen and felt; and

Father Hamilton assures me there is much of charm and influence in the woman's life, which I have not been able to see and feel. The ladies all seem busy, brisk, content; and those to whom I have spoken on this point, all say they are very happy in their lot. Perhaps there is one exception to the rule; that of a lady, whose name I shall not mention, as she dropt some hint that she might one day think of going home to her friends.

At first, the world waged war upon Oneida Creek, as it had done upon Putney; making jokes against free-love, loading pistols against community of goods. Noyes claims, not only in his contest with Baptist and Congregational preachers, but in his more dangerous conflicts with Madison farmers and herdsmen, that the kingdom of Christ established on Oneida Creek should be judged as a whole. The sexual principle, he says, is the helpmeet of the religious principle; and to all complaints from without, he answers, "Look at our happy circle; we work, we rest, we study, we enjoy: peace reigns in our household; our young men are healthy, our young women bright; we live well, and we do not multiply beyond our wishes!"

By time the enmity of the world has been overcome; the quicker since the world begins to see that the members of this community, though they may be wrong in their interpretation of the New Testament, are in real earnest as to living the word which they profess. Father Noyes is now popular in this neighbourhood, where the people judge his disciples by the results.

But a prophet may not waste his life upon a little farm, teaching his disciples by his own example how to live. Noyes finds that he has work to do on a larger scale and in a wider field: a new faith to expound, an intellectual conquest to achieve; and for these ends of his living as a witness, it is needful for him to reside a good deal in New York, at the centre of all moral, of all commercial, of all spiritual activities and agencies; where the Bible Family keep a store, and where The Circular is sold. Enough for him that he visits the two settlements of Wallingford and Oneida from time to time; received as a prophet, and implored, like the prophets of old, to mediate daily between man and God.

The Family at Oneida Creek consists of about three hundred members, a number which these Bible Communists say is found by trial to be large enough to foster and develope the graces and virtues which belong to a perfect Society. Applicants for admission are refused from day to day. Three or four offers to come in have been refused while I have been lodging at the Creek; the system of life here practised being simply regarded as experimental. The foundations, Father Noyes tells me, are now regarded as having been laid. When the details have been wrought out, other Families will be formed in New York and in the New England states.

Before I left Mount Lebanon I had some conversation with Elder Frederick about these people. "You may expect to see the Bible Families increase very fast," said Frederick, who looks upon their growth with anything but a friendly eye; "they meet the desires of a great many men and women in this country; men who are weary, women who are fantastic; giving, in the name of religious service, a free rein to the passions, with a deep sense of repose. Women find in them a great field for the affections. The Bible Communists give a pious charter to Free Love, and the sentiment of Free Love is rooted in the heart of New York."

## CHAPTER XXV.

#### Young America.

"We do not multiply beyond our wishes," said Noyes, in summary of the many beauties and advantages of what he and his people call the new Bible Order. "The baby question is the great question of the world," cried Brother Wright, among the Spiritualists of Providence. What do these reformers mean? In a score of different places, people have founded an annual baby-show at which they give prizes to the best specimen of baby-beauty; so many dollars (or the dollars' worth) for fine teeth, for bright eyes, for chubby cheeks, for fat arms and hands, and for a thousand nameless merits which a jury of ladies can assert in these rosy yearlings. What do these facts imply? Is infant beauty becoming rare? Has the public mind been roused to a consciousness of the decline? These things can hardly be: since Young America crows and laughs, and is quite as fat, as rosy, and hilarious, as either Young England or Young France. Do the facts suggest that babies are growing scarce on this American soil? If this were the case, a great many people would cry "Amen" to Brother Wright's announcement that the baby question is the chief question of these latter times!

Now, I have been told that one result of the

rapid growth in society and in the household of disturbing female creeds, is a fact, of which the wiser men and graver women of New England — the great majority of sound and pious people — think very much, though they seldom allude to it in public.

What I have seen and heard in this country, leads me to infer that there is a very strange and rather wide conspiracy on the part of women in the upper ranks — a conspiracy which has no chiefs, no secretaries, no head-quarters; which holds no meetings, puts forth no platform, undergoes no vote, and yet is a real conspiracy on the part of many leaders of fashion among women; the end of which — if the end should ever be accomplished — would be this rather puzzling fact: — there would be no more baby-shows in this country, since there would be no longer any Americans in America.

In Providence, the capital of Rhode Island, a model city in many ways — beautiful and clean, the centre of a thousand noble activities — I held a conversation on this subject with a lady, who took the facts simply as she said they are known to her in Worcester, in Springfield, in New Haven, in a hundred of the purest cities of America, and she put her own gloss and colour upon them thus: — "A woman's first duty is to look beautiful in the eyes of men, so that she may attract them to her side, and exert an influence over them for good; not to be a household drudge, a slave in the nursery, the kitchen, and the school-room. Everything that spoils a woman in this respect, is against her true interest, and she has a right to reject it, as a man would reject an impost that was being laid unjustly on his gains. A wife's first thought should be for her husband, and for herself as his companion in the world. Nothing should ever be allowed to come between these two." I ventured to ask the lady, her husband sitting by, whether children do come between father and mother; saying that I had two boys and three girls of my own, and had never suspected such a thing. "They do," she answered boldly; "they take up the mother's time, they impair her beauty, they waste her life. If you walk down these streets" (the streets of Providence) "you will notice a hundred delicate girls just blushing into womanhood; in a year they may be married; in ten years they will be hags and crones. No man will care for them, on the score of beauty. Their husbands will find no lustre in their eyes, no bloom upon their cheeks. They will have given up their lives to their children."

She spoke with fervour, and with a fixed idea that what she was saying to me might be said by any lady in open day before all the world; unconscious, as it seemed to me, that while proudly insisting on woman's rights, she and those for whom she spoke were ready to abandon all woman's duties; unconscious also, as it seemed to me, that in asserting the loss of beauty, as a consequence of domestic cares, she and those who think with her were assuming the very fact which almost every father, almost every husband, would deny. Yet, in pious Boston and Philadelphia, no less than in wicked

New Orleans and New York, this objection to become a mother in Israel is one of those radical facts which (I am told) must be admitted, whether for good or evil; the rapid diminution of native-born persons being matter of record in many public acts. What my Saratoga friend said to me about his countrywomen having no descendants left alive in a hundred years, expresses the fears of many serious men.

Now, this assertion of the growing scarcity of native-born children in the United States will probably be new and strange to many; since, in England, we are constantly hearing, in the first place, of the rapid growth of the population in America, as compared with Europe; and, in the second place, of the high value which is set in that new country on every individual child. In some districts, also, the rule which we find in the New England States, and among the higher classes in Pennsylvania and New York, is not observable. In Ohio and Indiana, and generally, indeed, in the western country, the female prides herself on her brood of darlings, and the Missouri boss, not having a fine lady for a wife, rejoices in his regiment of stalwart sons. Here, in New England, in New York, it is wholly different from what we see in yon healthy and vigorous western cities. It may be only fashion, it may be only frenzy, but for the passing moment, America (I am told) is wasting for the want of mothers. In the great cities, among those shoddy queens who live in monster hotels, among those nobler ladies who live in their own houses, it is extremely rare to find a woman who has such a brood of romping boys and girls about her as an ordinary English mother is proud to give her country. The rule as to number of offspring is rather that of Paris than that of London.

On a point of so much delicacy, I should wish to be understood as speaking with all reserve, and subject to a happy correction of any unconscious errors. A stranger must not expect to see down into all the depths of this mystery of domestic life. Ladies may be shy of debating such topics, and with men who are not their physicians, it is right that they should abstain from conveying their creed by hints. But the fact that many of these delicate and sparkling women do not care to have their rooms full of rosy darlings is not a matter of inference. Allusions to the nursery, such as in England and Germany would be taken by a young wife as compliments, are here received with a smile, accompanied by a shrug of undoubted meaning. You must not wish an American lady, in whose good graces you desire to stand, many happy returns of a christening day; she might resent the wish as an offence; indeed, I have known a young and pretty woman rise from a table and leave the room, on hearing such a favour expressed towards her by an English guest.

Now, what, if this is true, can be the end of such a fashion among the upper classes, except the rapid displacement of the old American stock? Statesman, patriot, moralist, here is a question to engage your thoughts! The Irish and the Germans rush into every vacant place. Is it pleasant for any one to consider that in three or four generations more there may be no Americans left on the American soil? In the presence of such a possibility, have the many noble churches, the many conservative schools of New England no mission to assume?

The tale which seems to be so sadly written on the floor of every room you enter, is also told at large in the census returns. Where are the American States in which the birth-rate stands the highest in proportion to the number of people? Is it found highest in pious New Hampshire, in moral Vermont, in sober Maine? All fancies, all analogies, would have led us to expect it; but the facts are wholly out of keeping with conjecture. In these three pious, moral, and sober states, the birth-rate is lowest. The only states in which there is a high and healthy rate of natural increase, are the wild countries peopled by new settlers, — Oregon, Iowa, Minnesota, Mississippi, — states in which, it is said, there are few fine ladies and no bad fashions. Strangest of all strange things is the example set to the rest of these States by Massachusetts, the religious centre of New England, the intellectual light of the United States. In Massachusetts, the young women marry; but they seldom become mothers. The women have made themselves companions to their husbands; brilliant, subtle, solid companions. At the same time the power of New England is passing over to the populous West, and a majority of the rising generation of Boston is either of German or of Irish birth.

This rather dismal prospect for Young America is not a consequence of the Germans and Irish put together exceeding the natives in number. Those nationalities are large no doubt; but as yet they have not turned the scale. The list of marriages still exhibits a preponderance of natives; and it is only when you come to the register of births that the account runs all another way.

Under the constitution of the United States, numbers are strength; numbers make the laws; numbers pay the taxes; numbers vote away the land. Power lies with the majority; and the majority in Massachusetts is going over to the Irish poor; to the Fenian circles and the Molly Maguires. At present the foreigners count only one in five; but as more children are being born to that foreign minority than to the native majority, the proportions are changing every year. In twenty years, those foreign children will be the majority of men in Massachusetts.

How will the intellectual queens of Boston bear the predominance of such a class?

## CHAPTER XXVI.

#### Manners.

"What *do* you think of this country?" said to me an English lady, who had spent two years of her life in the middle states, Ohio and Kentucky. Though I had then been five whole days in New York, I had not come to a final judgment on the virtues of thirty millions of people; so I answered my friend with a cowardly evasion, that it seemed to me a free country. "Free!" cried the lady, with a shrug; "you are fresh to it now: when you have lived here three or four months I shall be glad to learn what you have seen and thought. Free! The men are free enough; but then, what *they* call their freedom, *I* should style their impudence."

Those words are often in my thoughts; never more than they have been to-day, while strolling through these streets of Philadelphia, now that I have fulfilled my terms and travelled over ten thousand miles of American ground. A lady fresh from May Fair, used only to the ways of well-bred men, to the silent service of her maid and groom, would be sure to fall, like my questioner, into the error of supposing that the only liberties to be found in America are the liberties which people take with you.

All men of Teutonic race are apt to cast big looks on the strangers whom they meet by chance. It is a habit of our blood. The Norse gods had it; and we, their heirs, can hardly ever see an unknown face, an unfamiliar garb, without feeling in our hearts the longing to hoot and pelt. In presence of a strange man, a gentleman puts on his armour of cold disdain, a rough looks out for a convenient stone.

We bear this impulse with us on our journeys to and fro about the earth, Englishmen carrying it in the form of pride, Americans in the form of brag. Of course, it is not the way with all. Men of large hearts, of wide experience, of gentle nurture, will neither wrap their pride in an offensive coldness, nor obtrude their power in a boastful phrase. But some of the rank and file, having neither large hearts, nor wide experience, nor gentle nurture, will always do so; enough of them, perhaps, to create in a stranger's mind the impression that this English reserve, this Yankee brag, are notes of the Anglo-Saxon race. I shall not say which of these two methods of announcing our riches, gifts, titles, powers, and possessions — our strength, our glory, our superiority — is the more galling to men of another stock; Italians and Frenchmen tell me they have given the palm of offence to our haughty and unbending pride. A Yankee says to them plainly, either in word or look: "I am as good as you are — better;" they know the worst at once. An Englishman says nothing; they have no defence against him; and his silence is both galling and intrusive. Now, we English are apt to judge American shortcomings very much as Frenchmen and Italians judge our own, with the addition of a family pique; so that our cousins of this other side come out from such trials of their imperfections very much tattered and torn.

In an old country like England, where society is stronger than among our cousins in this new home — where personal fancies are held in check by public sentiment, acting in the name of fashion — ordinary men and women are apt to consider smoothness of surface, softness of voice, conformity of style, as of higher moment than they would appear to judges of the stamp of Mill. Of course, no man of the world, even though he should happen to be a philosopher, will despise the charms of a good manner. The lady who sits next to me at dinner, being well dressed, speaking in low tones, eating her food daintily, smiling on occasion sweetly, does me, by her presence, a positive service. The gentleman across the table, who is always telling the company, in looks and tones, that he is as good as they are — better than they are — takes all flavour from the dish, all bouquet from the wine. Manners may be no more than the small circulating coinage of society; but when these bits of silver have the true mint-mark upon them, they will pass for all that they are worth in every place, at every hour of the day. In the moment of a quick demand a few cents in the purse may be of higher value to a man than a bag of dollars laid up in a bank. What makes a good manner of so much worth as to have raised it into one of the fine arts, is the fact that in the free commerce of men and women, none but the minor debts of society are likely to arise between guest and guest. In the street, in the hotel, in the railway-train, a man's character hardly ever comes into play. What a man is may be of little account to the passer-by; what he does may either gladden that passer-by with delightful thoughts, or torture him into agonies of shame.

The Yankee of our books and farces — the man who was for ever whittling a yard of stick, putting his heels out of window, grinding his quid of pig-tail, squirting his tobacco-juice in your face, while, in breathless and unsuspecting humour, he ran, to your amazement and amusement, through a string of guesses, reckonings, and calculations, as to what you were, whence you came, what you were doing, how much money you were worth — as to whether you were single or married, how many children you had, what you thought of everything, and whether your grandmother was alive or dead — that full embodiment of the great idea of Personal Freedom is not so common and so lively as he would seem to have been some twenty years ago. Seeking for him everywhere, finding a shadow of him only, and that but seldom, I have missed him very much; an element of extravagance and humour that would have been very welcome to me in long, grave journeys, which were often a thousand miles in silence. In the waggon from Salt Lake to Kearney, in the boat from Omaha to St. Louis, in the car from Indianapolis to New York, I have often longed for the coming of one of those vivacious rattles, who used (as we have read) to poke his stick into your ribs, his nose into your conversation, to tell you everything he didn't know, and to pull out your eye-teeth generally; but he no more came in answer to my wish than the witty cabman comes in Dublin, the stolid Pasha in Damascus, the punctilious Don in Madrid — those friends of our imagination, whom we love so much on paper, and whom we never meet in our actual lives!

In the room of this lost humourist, you find at your elbow in the car, in the steamboat, at the dinner-table, a man who may be keen and bright, but who is also taciturn and grave; asking few questions, giving curt answers; a man occupied and reserved; on the whole, rather English in his silence and his pride than Yankee (of the book pattern) in his loquacity and his smartness. Perhaps he whittles; perhaps he chews; assuredly he spits. What impels a man to whittle when he is busy — while he is planning a campaign, composing an epic, mapping out a town? Is it an English habit, lost to us at home, like rocking in arm-chairs and speaking through the nose? I hardly think so. Is it a relic of some Indian custom? The Algonquins used to keep their reckonings by means of cuts and notches on a twig; and when Pocohontas came to England, her followers brought with them a bundle of canes, on which they were to keep accounts of what they saw among the Pale-faces. Whittling may be a remnant of this Indian custom; and the gentleman resting on the next bench to me, without a thought of Pocohontas and her people, may be whittling notes for his election speeches on his stick. I wonder whether he learned to chew at school? I wonder how he felt when he first put pig-tail into his mouth?

In a railway-train, in a ball-room, in the public street, you have much to do with a man's habits and behaviour, not much with his virtues and acquirements. In my journey from Columbus to Pittsburg, I spent about twenty hours in company with a Missouri boss. Now a boss is a master (the word is Dutch, and has gone westward from New York). In London he would have been a capitalist, in Cairo an effendi; in one city he would have had the bearing of a gentleman, in the other he would have had the aspect of a prince. He was a good fellow, as I came to know; but he made no approach in his dress, in his speech, in his bearing, to that elegant standard which in Europe denotes the gentleman. A fine lady would not have touched him with her fan.

Whence comes that nameless grace of style, — that tender and chivalric bearing, which, in rounding off all angles, smoothing away all knots, makes a man appear lovely and acceptable in the eyes of all his fellows? Is it an affair of race? We English have it only in degree; a little more perhaps, naturally, than the Dutch. It is a gift that never comes to us easily and at once; we have to toil for it long, and we seldom win it when we try. No man, says an old adage, has a fine accent, an easy carriage, a perfect presence, whose grandmother was not a lady born; for in society, as in heraldry, it takes three generations of men to make a gentleman. Thus in our common speech, we imply by a good manner a gentle descent, and by the term high breeding we express our sense of personal charm.

But this common use of language fails to express and explain the action of a general rule. Among Gothic tribes, in whom the tendency towards individual freak is strong, this outward and conceding softness of demeanour may be slow to come and swift to go; it may only come to men who have ease and leisure, brightened by moral culture, and by intellectual toil. In the Latin, in the Greek, in the Arab, it would almost seem as though it required no time to grow, no effort to improve. An Italian rustic has often a finer manner than an English earl. Why is this so? Not because country habits are a liberal education, as the poets feign; an English plough-boy having no rival in Europe for gross stupidity and awkwardness, unless he can find his mate in that Dutch peasant, whose name of "boor" has passed into our language as the fullest expression for lout and clown. Even the Italian, elegant as his bearing always is, cannot stand in comparison with the more supple Greek. A native of Athens, Smyrna, Rhodes, will fleece you with a grace that more than half inclines you to forgive him for the cheat. But he, again, must yield the palm before the easy and unstudied beauty of an Arab's mien; a man whose every gesture is a lesson in the highest of social arts. When you are in an Eastern city, even in an Eastern desert, the question is for ever springing to your lips — who taught you muleteer to bow and smile? who gave that fluent grace to yon tawny Sheikh? A lady, coming into an Arab's camp at night, would feel no dread, unless she had been warned by previous trials: for the Sheikh, under whose canvas tent she may find herself, has, in a perfection rarely seen, that gift of gait and speech which in the west is only to be sought, not always to be found, in men of the highest rank. How does the Bedouin gain this princely air? Not from his wealth and power — a herd of goats, a flock of sheep, are his sole estate; not from his mental efforts — he can hardly read and write. The Sheikh who inspires this confidence, so far from being a prince, a priest, bound by his nature and his habit to do right, may be a thief, an outlaw, an assassin, after his kind, with the scorch of fire and the stain of blood upon that hand which he waves with a bewitching grace. Yet he looks the prince. All Orientals have this nameless charm. A Syrian peasant welcomes you to his stone hut, makes his sign of the cross, and hopes that "Peace will be with you," after a fashion which a caliph could not mend. Ease is the element in which he lives; grace seems to have become his second nature; and he moves with the dignity of his high-born mare.

When you quit the East, you leave some part of that fine air, that flattering courtesy, behind you. Less of it is found in Alexandria than in Cairo; less in Smyrna than at Damascus. Sailing westward, you will lose it more and more; by a scale of loss that might be measured on a chart. Speaking roundly, the gift of seeming soft and gracious, which we call by the name of Manner, declines in a regular order from East to West; in Europe, it is best in Stamboul, worst in London; in the world (so far as I have seen), it is best in Cairo, worst at Denver and Salt Lake. And the rule which governs the ends of these great chains, holds good for all the links between them; the finer courtesies of life being more apparent in St. Louis than Salt Lake; in New York than in St. Louis; in London than in New York; in Paris than in London; in Rome than in Paris; in Athens than in Rome; in Stamboul than in Athens; in Cairo and Damascus than in Stamboul. If I ever go westward to California, I shall expect to find the manners worse in San Francisco than they are at St. Louis and Salt Lake.

## CHAPTER XXVII.

#### Liberties.

WILL any one learned in the ways of nature say what is the cause of a decline in manners which may be noted at every stage of a journey from the Usbeyah to Pennsylvania Avenue? What is the secret of the art itself? Whence comes this gentle craft, of which the Saxon has so little, the Persian has so much? Man for man, a Persian is less noble than an Arab, an Arab than a Gaul, a Gaul than a Briton; why then should the lower race excel the higher in this subtle test of bearing? Is manner nothing more than a name for the absence of liberty? Is that soft reserve, that bated voice, that deprecating tone, no more than a sacrifice of individual force to social order? Are we polite because we are not ourselves? In short, is a good manner a liberal accomplishment or only a slavish grace?

Two facts may be taken as proved. 1. This charm has scarcely any affection for busy commonwealths. No free people has much of it to spare; no servile nation is without it in abundance. In America, the Negro has it, the Cheyenne has not; in Europe, the Greek has more of it than the Gaul; in Asia, the Persian and Hindoo have more of it than the Armenian and the Turk. 2. It is rarely found among men of the highest genius. Whether in arts or letters manner means mediocrity; mannerism of style is but a name for the absence of individuality, of invention, of original power. Men who show great force of character cannot show a fine manner, which implies polish, smoothness, and conformity. Hence, men of the higher genius are called eccentrics and originals.

Might not a rule be laid down which should express an approach to the truth in some such words as these: a people has this exceeding grace of spirit in exact proportion to the length and strength of the despotism under which it has been schooled?

I do not say that such will be found the final form of this rule. As yet we have few materials, and no fixed principles, for a science of the Life of Man. But if a large experience and induction were at some future time to show that such is the truth, the fact would serve to explain some points which in our present state of knowledge give us no great pleasure. Men of poetic habits, when they hear of nations falling off in manners as they gain in liberty and power, are apt to grieve, and almost to despair. That nations do fall off in manners with the advance of freedom and prosperity is one of those facts which are open, obvious, uniform; written in every figure, told in every glance. Go where you list, from Jerusalem to Florence, from Paris to New York, the tale is everywhere the same. The Effendine families in Zion are noticed as being far less affable, now that, after Arab measure, they are rich and free, than when the Holy City was an Arab camp, governed by a pasha of two tails, administering his rough injustice in the Jaffa gate. A Greek is far less winsome in his ways, less sweet and pleasant to have about you, now that he has ceased to be a slave. The Roman Jew, so smoothly spoken, so obsequious to your wish, in the days of yore, has now put on a saucy and audacious air. Free Florence has lost her name for sweet and tender courtesy since she has ceased to gaze into the Austrian's eyes, and make humble love to the Austrian's boot. France threw down her repute for bows and smiles, when she rose up in her wrath to slay her tyrants and break her chains. Yes, with the growth of liberty the school of manners seems to be everywhere decaying. A Suabian is less polite in Omaha than in Augsburgh; a Munster man in Baltimore than in Cork. Fritz will not say Good Evening to you on Lake Erie, Pat will not touch his cap to you in New York. Are not these changes the result of general laws? And if they be, what are those laws?

If it should appear that the fine flavour which we call manner is but a note and sign of long submission to a master's will, you may find in the fact some grain of consolation even when a passing rowdy squirts his tobacco on your boots. This negro at the corner will brush them clean; doing his service for you with a soft alacrity, a submissive laughter, to charm your heart. Yesterday, this fellow was a slave, subject to cuffs and stripes, compelled to cringe and fawn. His son will have a way of his own; and his son's son, with a vote at the poll, a balance at the bank, will not be found so meek in spirit as to lie in the dust at your descendant's feet. Like every free man born on this American soil he will probably say in gait and tone, "Ask me not to serve you, am I not as good as you?"

It is well to know that the rough liberties for which our cousins have exchanged, as a rule, the deferential habits of their fathers, are of a solid and fruitful kind. If they have sold their birthright of civility, they have not sold it for a mess of pottage. Indeed, they may be said to have made a very good market of their manners; having got in return for them houses, votes, schools, wages; a splendid present for themselves, a magnificent future for their children. They have risen in society; they have ceased to be servants.

The relation of a French cook, of an English butler, of a Swiss valet, to his master, is a thing unknown in this country, whether you search for it on the Ohio, on the Delaware, on the sea-shore. Here you have no masters, no servants. No native white will serve another. Ask your friends in Richmond, in New York, about the birthplace of their domestics; you will find that their serving men and serving women are all either Irish or negro. A lady cannot get a native maid, her husband cannot get a native groom. Tempt a street huckster with as many dollars as would buy you a dozen clerks, and the chances are many that he will say: "I am as good as you; I have the same vote as you; I can go into Congress as well as you; I may be President as soon as you;" and the facts as between you and him are mainly as he puts them. A working tailor lives at the White House. One of the most popular Presidents since

Washington died, was a log-clearer, a woodsman. In this free country all careers lie open. They have always been so in yon Northern States; and since the War this Northern rule is fast becoming the law for every part. Even in Virginia there will soon be no mean whites. In Ohio birth is nothing; in Cincinnati, I have heard it said, that no man has any need for a grandmother. Each man must make himself. Nor does it greatly matter what a man has been some dozen years ago; one year is an age in this swift country; indeed, this liberal dealing runs to such excess, that if a fellow has a smooth tongue, and keeps himself clean, the fact of his having passed a term in Auburn will not weigh heavily on his neck. Morrisey, the New York gambler, once a pugilist, then a prisoner, afterwards a faro-banker, may wear white kid, and give his vote in the Capitol. To pluck, to enterprise, to genius, every office in the land is open prize.

No white native, therefore, need despair so far as to sink into the grade of servant: the position, as he would call it, of a stranger and a slave. If he should fall so low, he would be lost for ever in the minds of his former friends, like a Brahman who had forfeited his caste.

Nor do you find among these free citizens of the Great Republic much of that show of deference which in France and England would be understood, on both sides, as the expectation of a silver coin. No native American ever takes a vail. A driver in the street may cheat you, but he will not take from you a cent beyond his claim. No porter will accept a gift for service; no messenger will accept a reward for haste. Sometimes a news-boy will object to receiving change out of a greenback; more than once I have had my couple of cents thrown back into my lap. Thus it happens that no one ever proffers help in your little straits; for no one being employed in looking out for doles, your trouble is not his affair. When you are either young to the country, or careless of its ways, you may have to fetch water to your room, lift your box into the car, take your letter to the post; in short, do every little act for yourself which would be done for you in London for a shilling, in Paris for a franc. Where no man needs your vails, no man watches to do you good. Help yourself — this is a stranger's motto and necessity in these free States.

Perhaps, the liberty which is more than any other likely to amuse a traveller in this country, is the freedom with which every one helps himself to anything he may want. In a railway car, anybody who likes it will sit down in your place, push away your satchel, seize upon your book. Thought of asking your leave in the matter may not occur to him for hours. I lent a book to a man in the car at St. Louis; he kept it two days and nights; and then asked me if I was reading it myself. On my saying yes, he simply answered, "It is amusing; you will have a good time." On the Pennsylvania central line, a lady entered into my state-room, on pretence of looking out upon a river; she kept my seat, for which I had paid an extra fare, until her journey ended. If you ask for any dish at dinner, your neighbour, should the fancy take him, will snatch a portion of it from beneath your nose. When I was leaving Salt Lake City, Sister Alice, the daughter of Brigham Young, put up some very fine apples in a box for me to eat by the way; at a station on the Plains I found that a lady, a fellow-passenger in the waggon, had been opening my box, and helping herself to the fruit; and when she saw me looking at her, with some surprise perhaps visible on my face, she merely said, "I am trying whether your apples are better than mine." In the western country, a man will fire off your pistols, try on your gauntlets. Any one thinks himself at liberty to clean his clothes with your brushes, run his hair through your comb, and warm himself in your great-coat.

These things are not meant to be offensive. A fellow gives and takes; lends you a buffalo-hide on a frosty night; helps himself to your drinking-cup at the morning well. The manner is not fine; but the heartiness is pleasant, and you would be unintelligible if you made complaint. Every one you meet has the way which in Europe would be called original.

## CHAPTER XXVIII.

### Law and Justice.

When Secretary Seward put to me the question which every American puts to an Englishman travelling in the United States, "Well, sir, what do you think of our country?" I ventured to reply, partly at least in jest, "I find your country so free that nobody seems to have any rights." As in all such sayings, there was some exaggeration in these words; yet they convey an impression dwelling on my mind.

No men in the world, not even we English, from whom they derive the virtue, boast so constantly, and with so much reason, of being a law-loving, a law-abiding people as these Americans. Having no State religion, no authentic Church, they seem to cling to the written Law, whether it be that which was fixed by the Constitution, that which has been voted by Congress, or only that which is defined by the Supreme Court, as to a rock in the midst of storm.

Few things in this free country stand above the reach of cavil. That light which in Europe is said to beat upon a throne, here beats upon every object, whether high or low. Nothing can be done in secret; no one is permitted to live in private. Every man drives in a glass coach, and every body flings a stone at him as he dashes past. Censure is the world's first duty; in some societies, such as the Bible Communists', criticism is adopted as the only governing power. Life is a Broadway procession. From the elegant frivolities of a lady's boudoir in Madison Square, down to the midnight follies enacted in the cellars of the Louvre, everything in yon city of New York is known, is seen, is judged by public opinion. The pulpit is accused, the press suspected, the government condemned. Capital is assailed and enterprise is watched. Each man thinks for himself, judges for himself, about the most delicate, the most sacred things — love, marriage, property, morality, religion. Law and justice do not always escape this rage for popular debate; but by common assent of minds, they are regarded as the very last subjects to be handled, and only then to be touched with reverential hand.

Whether it be constitutional, general, state, or only municipal, Law is nobly respected by the native American. The Judge of the Supreme Court is treated in Washington with a degree of respect unknown to lawyers in Europe; a respect akin to that which is paid to an archbishop in Madrid and to a cardinal in Rome. The State Judges take the places in society held among us by bishops. Even the village justice, though he is elected by the crowd, is always styled the squire.

This deference to the Law, and to every one who wears the semblance of lawful authority, is so complete in America, as to occasion a traveller some annoyance and more surprise. Every dog in office is obeyed with such unquestioning meekness, that every dog in office is tempted to become a cur. It is rare, indeed, to find a servant of the public civil and obliging. He may be something better, but assuredly he is neither helpful nor deferential. A news-boy will not serve you with a "Ledger," an "Inquirer," unless he likes. A policeman hardly condescends to show you the nearest way. A railway-guard will put you in this car, in that car, among the ladies, among the rowdies, among the smokers, just as he lists. A crowd of busy and free Americans will stand about, and bear this insolence of authority with a shrug, saying they cannot help it. When coming up from Richmond by the night train, Mr. Laurence Oliphant, myself, and many more, arrived at Acquia Creek about one o'clock; the passage thence to Washington takes four hours; and as we were much fatigued, and had only these four hours for rest, we begged that the keys of our berths might be given to us at once. "I'll attend to you when I'm through," was the only answer we could get; and we waited — a train of ladies, young folks, gentlemen — until the man had arranged his affairs, and smoked his pipe, more than an hour. Yet not one word was said, except by Mr. Oliphant and myself. The man was in office; excuse enough in American eyes for doing as he pleased. This is the kind of circle in which they reason; take away his office, and the man is as good as we are; all men are free and equal; add office to equality, and he rises above our heads. More than once I have ventured to tell my friends, that this habit of deferring to law and lawful authority, good in itself, has gone with them into extremes, and would lead them, should they let it grow, into the frame of mind for yielding to the usurpation of any bold despot who may assail their liberties, like Cæsar, in the name of law and order!

Sometimes, this profound respect for Law gives rise to singular situations. I may name two cases, one of which was told me at Clear Creek, near Denver, the other in Cass Township, Pennsylvania.

Black Bear, a Cheyenne warrior, who had scalped a white man, was arrested by the people of Denver. Across the English border he would have been tried on the spot and hung, there being no doubt whatever about his guilt; but the American people have such lofty regard for the forms of justice, that they will not suffer a murderer to be tried for his life, except under all the delicate conditions of a white man's court. Black Bear was brought from Colorado to Washington, two thousand miles from the scene of his crime; he had clever counsel to defend him; and the chief witnesses of his crime being far away, the jury gave him the benefit of all their doubts. Acquitted by the court, he became a lion in the city, especially among romantic women. He was taken to the Indian bureau; he was allowed to shake hands with the President; pistols and belts were given to him; and he returned to the Cheyenne camp a big chief, appearing to his own people to have been decorated and promoted by the white men, for no other cause than that of having taken their brother's scalp.

William Dunn, of Cass Township, Pottsville, was a manager of mines for the New York and Schuylkill Company; a gentleman and a man of science, with a great command over the coalfields of that picturesque and prosperous region of Pennsylvania. I have spent some days in that fine district, where I heard this story from the lips of his successor. Dunn was going about his duty, in the public street, in open day, when an Irish workman met him face to face, and with an insolent gesture asked for a holiday. "You cannot have it," said Dunn; "go back to your work." Without a word more, the Irishman drew a pistol from his belt and shot him dead. The murderer, taken red-handed, in the public street, standing by the body of his victim, was brought to trial in Pottsville, and — acquitted. In that great coalfield, with towns and cities which have grown up in the forest in a dozen years, the Irish are sixty thousand strong. They are very poor, they are grossly illiterate; but every man has a vote, and the sixty thousand vote together as one man. Hence they carry all elections in the coalfield; elect the judges, serve on the juries, control the courts. Among these men there is a secret society called The Molly Maguires, the name and habits of which they have introduced from Ireland. The judge who tried this murderer was elected by the Molly Maguires; the jurors who assisted him were themselves Molly Maguires. A score of Molly Maguires came forward to swear that the assassin was sixty miles from the spot on which he had been seen to fire at William Dunn. Counsel submitted that this was one of the many cases of mistaken identity which adorn our legal annals; the judge summed up the case in the spirit of this suggestion; and the jurors instantly returned a verdict of Not Guilty. That ruffian is still alive. The great company whose servant had been slain could do nothing but engage another in his place. One gentleman to whom they offered the post, replied that he would not take it unless he could be armour-plated.

When you speak of this case to the eminent men of the Pennsylvania bar they answer that these people cannot be punished, and that you must wait and work for a better state of things. "These criminals," they say, in substance, "are not Americans; they come to us from Europe; squalid, ignorant, brutal, they drink, they quarrel, they form secret associations; in their own country they paid their rent with a blunderbuss, in this country they ask for a holiday with a pistol, and demand an advance of wages with a blazing torch. But what are we to do? Can we close our ports against these immigrants? Should we change our judicial system, the pride of thirty-six millions of solid and steadfast people, to punish a mob of degraded Irish peasants?" So they allege, with a noble confidence in moral growth, that this evil must be left to cure itself; as they reckon it will do in five-and-twenty years. "The children of these Molly Maguires," says the keen and brilliant mayor of Philadelphia, Morton M'Michael, "will be decent people; we shall put them through our schools and train them in our ways; their children, again, will be rich and good Americans, who will hardly have heard of such a society as the Molly Maguires."

## CHAPTER XXIX.

#### Politics.

Society is made and held together by the poise and balance of two radical powers in man — akin to those centrifugal and centripetal forces which compel the planets to revolve about the sun — the separating spirit of freedom and the combining spirit of union.

Always acting, and in opposite ways, these forces hold each other in check; that shaking masses into units, this drawing units into masses; and it is only in their nice adjustment to each other that a nation can enjoy political life in the midst of social peace.

In all living men, these powers of separation and attraction are nearly equal, like the corresponding forces in all moving matter; but some races of men have a little more of the first power, others have a little more of the second power. The Latin race has a quicker sense of union than the Gothic race; the Gothic race has a keener love of liberty than the Latin race. Each may be capable of uniting public order with personal independence; but the paths by which they will separately arrive at such an end, diverging from the common line, will reach their goal by loops and zig-zags hardly perceptible to each other. A Latin people will dread the liberty for which it longs; a Gothic people will distrust the government of its choice. Compare the structure of a Teutonic Church with that of the Roman Church; compare the political life of America with that of France! Rome has a compactness of organization, to which neither London, Augsburg, nor Geneva can attain; while London, Augsburg, and Geneva have a freedom to which Rome cannot even aspire.

In France, again, the tendency of public thought, not of a school, of a party only, but of the solid people, is to sustain authority against the demands of personal right; in America, on the contrary, the action of all political bodies, of all colleges and corporations, of all private teachers, agitators, and philosophers, is directed, now consciously, now unconsciously, towards weakening the public force in favour of individual rights. France has not lost her love of liberty, nor America forgotten her respect for law; for these are elementary instincts in the human heart; without which, in some form of combination and adjustment, society, as we understand it, could not be. But in the large results of thought, in the wide action of politics, one nation is always tending towards military rule, the second nation towards popular rule; France seeking safety in the drill, the discipline, the armaments of a camp; America in the agitations of a pulpit, in the explosions of a press, in which every man has an unlicensed right of speech and thought.

Each of these tendencies implies a peril of its own. If the Latin is apt to sacrifice independence to empire, the Teuton is no less apt to sacrifice empire to independence. In France, the danger lies in too much compression — in America it lies in too much separation — of the political units.

For twenty years before the War broke out, the tendency of men in the United States towards separation had been excessive; not in one society, but in all societies; not in one body, but in all bodies; not between race and race only, but between men of the same race; not in the states only, but in the churches; not in politics and religion only, but in science, in literature, in social life. Until the War came down upon the nation like a judgment, rousing it from a trance, the moral atmosphere of America had been charged with the fire of secession; almost every man of intellectual force and native genius in the country, either being, or seeming to be, driven by the force of some inward spring from his obedience to natural rules and national laws. Society rights, class rights, property rights, — state rights, county rights, township rights, — land rights, mining rights, water rights, — church rights, chapel rights, temple rights, — personal rights, sexual rights — the rights of labour, of divorce, of profession — the rights of polygamy, of celibacy, of pantagamy — negro rights, Indian rights, equal rights, woman's rights, babies' rights: these are but samples of the names under which a common sentiment of division had taken shape and grown into an actual power. What man of mark then raised his voice for unity? Who cared for the central government unless he could mint it into dollars, turn it into patronage and power? Who taught the poor to feel reverence for the law? Were the rich, the learned, the intellectual members of this proud community ever seen in those days at yonder White House? What poet, what scholar, what divine, then made it his religion to respect a freedom which was guarded and controlled by the general vote? A man of genius here and there took office, chiefly in some foreign city; going far away from his native soil, to a place in which he could forget his country, while he made a tale, a poem, a morality of the messages and memories of a foreign race and a distant age. Irving went to the Alhambra. Bancroft sailed for London. Rich amused himself in Paris. Hawthorne mused in Liverpool; Motley pored over papers at the Hague. Power migrated to Florence, Mozier and Story pitched their tents in Rome. Longfellow, dallying with the Golden Legend, seemed to have forgotten the poetic themes which lay about his home. No one seemed to appreciate American scenery, no one appeared to value American law. For a moment everything brightest in the land lay under an eclipse.

Not a few of the more brilliant men — the younger lights of the New England schools — renounced their citizen rights, and even while they yet lived in Massachusetts, in Connecticut, in Rhode Island, declared themselves by a public act set free from all future loyalty to the United States. It is said that Ripley, Dana, Hawthorne, Channing, Curtis, Parker, some or all, laid down their common rights in the American courts, when they undertook to raise a new society at Brook Farm. Boyle, Smith, and Noyes, were only three in a thousand clever men — born in New England, nurtured in its societies, educated in its schools, licensed to preach its gospels — who seceded from the Great Republic; mocking its defenders, and contemning its institutions. "Ha!" roared Noyes, the idol-breaker, "do you fancy that heaven is a republic, that a majority governs in the skies, that angelic offices are elective, that God is a president, that His ministers are responsible to a mob?" And the crowds who heard him answered — No!

In the church it was much the same as in the political field. That old and stately church which has the root of its life in the mother country, has long ago ceased to be the popular church of America, if numbers may be taken as a certain test of power: but even this church of an upper class, of an aristocracy, rich, decorous, educated, had not been able wholly to escape that rage for rending and dividing which possessed its neighbours. The preachers struck, so to speak, for higher wages; when some of the laymen, hurt by a display of worldly motives, closely akin to those which govern affairs in Wall Street, quitted their fold for that of the Bible Communist, that of the Shaker, that of the Universalist.

The Wesleyan body, numerically the largest church in these States, parted into two great sects — a Methodist Episcopal Church North, and a Methodist Episcopal Church South; a division which was provoked, not caused, by the importance just then suddenly acquired by the negro question. In the northern section of the Methodist church, there was a further trouble and a second split, on account of conscientious scruples as to bishops' powers and laymen's rights; the latter point being mainly raised on the question whether Methodist laymen might sell rum. A new religious body, now of very great strength, the Wesleyan Methodist Church in the United States, grew out of this seccssion. Indeed, eight or nine sects have been formed out of the original church of Wesley and Whitfield, without counting those seceders who have gone out bodily from the rest.

Next in importance as to numbers come the Baptists; a body, like the Methodists, fired with holy zeal; which was found strong before the world, the flesh, the devil, yet weak in presence of this seceding spirit. In a very short time this body was divided into Old School Baptists (called by their enemies Anti-effort Baptists), Sabbatarians, Campbellites, Seventh-day German Baptists, Tunkers, Free-will Baptists, with their sub-section of Free Baptists; and into some minor parties.

In the Congregational Church, which prides itself on holding in its ranks the most highly educated ministers and professors in the United States, there are endless divisions, including Millennialists, Taylorites, and the strange heresy of the Perfectionists, founded by one of their students at Yale College. From the Millennialists, who fancied the world was about to end and the judgment to come, sprang the Millerites, who said it would end on a particular day. The Perfectionists, who declared that the world was already at an end, that the judgment had come down upon us, parted into Putneyites and Oberlinites; sects which threw dirt upon each other, and laughed and mocked when any of their opposing brethren fell into sin.

A great unrest invaded the retreat of the Moravian village of Bethlehem, in the pretty Lehigh mountains; where young men took to questioning book and law; until the Moravians of Pennsylvania lost some customs which had hitherto marked them as a peculiar church.

No sect escaped this rage for separation, for independence, for individuality; neither Unitarian, nor Omish, nor River Brethren, nor Winebrennarians, nor Swedenborgians, nor Schwenkfelders. Perhaps the Come-outers may be taken as the final fruit of this seceding spirit; since they separated themselves from the older churches, from the dead and dying churches, as they call them, for secession's sake, and solely in the hope of breaking down the religious bodies in which they had been reared. These Come-outers have two articles of faith: one social, one dogmatic; they believe that man and woman are equal, and that all the churches are dead and damned.

Society had to go through these trials; and she cannot be said to have got through her maladies without many a wound and scar; since, in the slackening of all ties and ligatures, men had begun to toy with some of her most sacred truths. Property was attacked. In the press, and in the pulpit, it was said that all private wealth was stolen from the general fund, that no one had a right to lay up riches, that no man could pretend to an exclusive holding in either wife or child. Doctors took up their parable against the sanctity of marriage; women began to doubt whether it was well for them to love their husbands and to nurse their children. Some ladies set the fashion of laughing at mothers; nay, it became in Boston, Richmond, and New York, a sign of high breeding to be known as a childless wife. Wretches arose in every city of the land, some of them men, more of them women, who professed to teach young wives the secret arts by which it is said, that in some old countries, such as France, the laws of nature have often been set aside. Many a great house is shown in New York, in which resided creatures of the night who imported into America this abominable trade.

Religion, science, history, morality, were thrust aside by these reformers, as clogs on individual liberty. What was a canon, a commandment, to a man resolved on testing everything for himself? Excess of freedom led a few to Communism, a few into Free-love. What, in truth, is this dogma of perfect freedom, except the right of every man to have his own will done, even though his will should take the form of wishing to possess his neighbour's house and his neighbour's wife? Some of these brave reformers, like Noyes and Maban, seized a religious feeling as the groundwork for their faith; others again, like the Owenites and Fourierites, made a scientific axiom serve their turn; while yet a third and more poetic class, the enthusiasts of Brook Farm, embraced a mystical middle term, making a god of Nature and of Justice. All these schools of practical socialists seceded from the world, renouncing in terms, either express or tacit, their allegiance to the United States.

What noble spirit, it was said, could suffer itself to be enslaved by canons, dogmas, precedents, and laws? Every man was now to be a law unto himself. Liberty was to have its day. The final stage of freedom, as it verges into chaos, is the stage in which no one has any rights left him to enjoy; and in many parts of America this stage of progress had, on the evening of the War, been nearly reached.

Family life was hardly less disturbed by this intruding spirit of separation; disputes arising on the domestic hearth, being carried into public meetings and female congresses, held to debate the most fanciful points of difference between male and female, husband and wife, parent and child. Women raised their voices against nursing babies, against the sanctity of wedlock, against the permanence of marriage vows. They asserted rights which would have grieved and puzzled such models of their sex as Lady Rachel Russel and Lady Jane Grey. Caroline Dall demanded that woman should have the right to labour in any profession she might care to adopt. Margaret Fuller taught her female readers to expect equality in the married state. Mary Cragin preached the doctrine of Free-love for woman, and practised what she preached. Eliza Farnham urged a revolt of woman against man, declaring that the female is intrinsically nobler than the male.

What a glorious strength of constitution this

young society must have had to endure with so little waste the shock of so many forces! What energy, what solidity, what stamina in the young Saxon republic!

## CHAPTER XXX.

#### North and South.

If the negro question lent a pretext to the rage of North and South, the cause of that strife in Charleston harbour which brought on civil war, lay closer to the core of things than any wish on the part of these southern gentry to maintain their property in slaves. The negro was a sign, and little more. Even that broader right of a state to live by its own lights — to make and unmake its laws — to widen or contract its enterprise — to judge of its own times and seasons — to act either with or without its fellow states — was but a pretext and a cry. The causes which have whitened these Virginian battle-fields (in the midst of which I write) lay deeper still. A planters' war could not have lived a month, a seceders' war could not have lived a year. The lists were drawn in another name, the passions welled from a richer source. No such beggarly stake as either of these engaged a million of English brothers in mortal strife. But when did nations ever close in combat with the actual cause of war emblazoned on their shields? Nations have a way of doing great things on poor grounds; of checking Russia in the name of a silver key, of making Italy on account of one hasty word. Men are the same in every clime. The prize for which the South contended against the

North, was nothing less than the Principle of National Life.

What idea should lie at the root of all social habits, all political creeds, in this great republic? In the constitution, itself a compromise, the make-shift of a day, this question had been left an open gap. Every year had seen that opening widen; and sagest men had often said, that such a question never could be closed, except in the old way, by a sovereign act of sacrifice.

On one side of a faint and failing line lay these Southern states, peopled for the most part by a race of Cavaliers; men brave and haughty, the representatives of privilege, education, chivalry; a class in whom the graces which come of birth, of culture, of command, had been developed to a high degree. On the other side of that line, lay yon Northern states, peopled for the greater part by men of Puritan descent; shrewd merchants, skilful artisans, the representatives of genius, enterprise, equality; a class in whom the virtues which spring from faith, ambition, and success, were all but universal.

Here stood the lotus-eater, with his airs and languors, his refinements and traditions; there stood the craftsman, with his head full of ideas, his heart full of faith, his arm full of strength. Which was to give the law to this Great Republic?

In the South, you had a gentle class and a servile class. One fought and ruled; one laboured and obeyed. Between these two sections of the Southern people yawned a mighty gulf,— a separating chasm of lineage, form, and colour; for the higher breed was of pure old English blood, offspring of men who had been the glories of Elizabeth's court; while the lower breed was of African descent, offspring of the mango plain and the ague swamp, children of men who had held the basest rank even among savages and slaves. No bridge could be thrown across that chasm. No touch of nature, it was thought, would ever be able to make the extremes of black and white of kin. In the eyes of their lords and ladies, — most of all in those of their ladies,—these coloured tenders of the rice-field and the cotton-plant were not men; they were only cattle, with the rights which belong to mules and cows; the right to be fed and lodged in return for work, and to be treated mercifully —after their kind. In many of these states the coloured people dared not learn to read and write; they could not marry, and hold on truly, man and wife, to each other; they had no control over their own children; they could not own either pigs, ducks, cows, or other stock; nor were they suffered to buy and sell, to hire out their labour, to use a family name. Against each other they had certain remedies for wrong; against the white man they had none. To use the sadly memorable phrase of Chief Justice Taney, a negro had no rights which a white man was bound to respect; in other words, he had none at all.

It is much to say that among men so tempted to abuse of power, there was less waste of life than in any other slave society, even on the American soil. Virginia was a paradise compared with Cuba and Brazil. Some touch of softness in the lord, some gleam of piety in the mistress, had sufficed to keep the very worst planters of English blood free from the brutalities which were daily practised in the Spanish and Portuguese cities farther south. Charleston was not a pleasant place for a negro slave; the law was not with him in his need; oftentimes he had to bear the bitter fruits of a tyrant's wrath. He was only too familiar with the lash, the chain, the blood-hound, and the gaol; but still, when weighed against the slave's condition in Havana, in Rio, in San Domingo, his life was that of a spoiled and petted child. The test of a people's happiness is the law of its reproduction. If a race is crushed beyond a certain point, nature protests against the wrong in her own emphatic way. The race declines. Now the negro has been dying away in every slave society on the American soil, save only on that which has been ruled by men of the Anglo-Saxon race. Bad as our rule, and that of our offshoots in Virginia and the Carolinas, may have been, the fact is legible on every part of this continent, in every island of the adjacent seas, that these English planters, and they alone, have given the African a chance of life. We put, from first to last, five hundred thousand negroes on the soil of our thirteen colonies; we made them toil and sweat for us; still, we treated them on the whole with so much mercy, that they are now nine times stronger, counting them by heads, than the number of their imported sires. In Spanish America, instead of the negroes of the present hour being nine times stronger than their fathers, they scarcely count one half the original tale. This is a little fact — recorded in a line; but what tragedies of woe and death it hides! When the great account is made up,—when all that we have done,—all that we have left undone,—is urged against us, may we not plead this increase of the negro under our dominion as some small set-off to our many sins?

A tourist from the Old World—one of the idler classes—found himself much at home in these country mansions. The houses were well planned and built; the furniture was rich; the table and the wine were good; the books, the prints, the music, were such as he had known in Europe. He found plenty of horses and servants; spacious grounds, fine woods, abundant game. In one place he got a little hunting; in a second place a little fishing. Nearly all the young ladies rode well, danced well, sang well. The men were frank, audacious, hospitable. What was unsightly in the place was either far away from a stranger's eyes, or made to look comical and picturesque. He heard of slavery as a jest, and went down to the plantation to see a play. Sam was called up before him to grin and yelp. A dance being on, and the can of punch going round as the negroes hopped and sang, he would go home from the scene merrily confused, and with an idea that the darkey rather loved his chains. In Missouri and Virginia I have seen enough to know how easily tourists may be deceived by the lightness and laughter of a negro crowd. A coloured man is plastic, loving, docile: for a kindly word, for a drink of whisky, for a moment's frolic, he will sing and dance. He is very patient, very slow. In Omaha

I found a rowdy beating a black lad in the street and inquired the cause:—"me say nigger have right to vote," said the lad; "dis gel'man say nigger aint folks nohow." The lad made no complaint of being beaten: indeed, he laughed as though he liked it. If the white man had been his master, he, too, would have smiled, and I should possibly have thought it a pretty jest.

The South was made pleasant to its English guest; for the people felt that the English were of nearer kin to them than their Yankee brethren. A sunny sky, a smiling hostess, an idle life, and a luxurious couch, led him softly to forget the foundations on which that seducing fabric stood.

In the Northern States such a lotus-eater would have found but little to his taste. The country-houses — except in the neighbourhood of Philadelphia, where the fine old English style is still in vogue — were not so spacious and so splendid as in the South; the climate was much colder; and the delights of lounging were much less. He had nothing to do, and nobody had time to help him. The men being all intent on their affairs, they neither hunted, fished, nor danced; they talked of scarcely anything but their mills, their mines, their roads, their fisheries; they were always eager, hurried, and absorbed, as though the universe hung upon their arms, and they feared to let it fall. The women, too, were busy with a care and trouble of their own. No idle mornings in the library, in the greenhouse, on the lawn, could be got from these busy creatures, who were gone from the breakfast-table to the school-room, to the writing-desk, to the sewing-frame, long before the guest had played out his fund of compliments and jokes. It was true that when they could be got to talk about science, politics, and letters, he found them read to the highest point — full of the last fact, the last movement, the last book; bright and knowing people, who let nothing pass them, and with the habit of turning their acquirements to instant use; sometimes making him do service in an unexpected way. But he, an idler in the land, had no enjoyment in their rapid talk. They thought of him little, of their own projects much. When he wanted only to loll and dream, his host had to meet a banker in the city, his hostess had to teach a class in the village-school. He must amuse himself, he was always being told, until the afternoon. There was the coal-mine to see, the new bridge to inspect, the steam-harrow to test. What did he care about coal, and bridge, and harrow! He would smoke a cigarette, and take the very next train for Richmond.

In these sunny Southern houses, with their long verandahs, their pleasant lawns, no man was busy, no woman was in haste. Every one had time for wit, for compliment, for small talk. The day went by in gossip. No man there ever thought of working, for to work was the slave's office. Work was ignoble in these cities. Society had said, "'Thou shalt not labour and escape the curse;" and white men would not put their hands to the plough. "Work!" said a stout young fellow in Tennessee to a man from whom he was asking alms, "thank God, I have never done a stroke of work since I was born; I am not going to change; you may hang me if you like, but you shall never make me work." In these sad words spoke the spirit of the South. "In one thing we were wrong," said to me a Georgian gentleman; "our pride would not let us teach. We had scarcely any professors in the South. Our people were well trained and grounded; we had some good scholars and more good speakers; but we had to send into our enemies' schools, to Cambridge and New Haven, for our teachers, whether male or female; and they almost taught our children to be Yankees." Teaching was work, and a Georgian could neither work nor recognise the dignity of work. In one of those passionate storms which sometimes swept across these languid cities, the evils of this borrowed life being clear, it was proposed to found a great University in the South, and to invite, by liberal chairs, the most eminent men of literature and science from Europe, and also from the North; amongst them, Prof. Agassiz, who was to have been installed their chief. "And how about our social standing?" asked the great professor, from whom I heard these details. There came the rub. The social standing of a teacher in the South! A teacher could not hope to hold any standing in the slave society, and thereupon the proposal to invite the best men to come over from Oxford and Berlin, as well as from Boston and New Haven, tumbled to the ground.

In the Northern cities you had neither a gentle class nor a servile class. In their stead you had men of learning, business, enterprise; men of as pure and lofty lineage as the Southern chivalry, with fresher notions, hardier habits, and a larger faith. The Middle Ages and the Modern Ages could not come together and live in peace; each would be master in the Great Republic — on the one side Chivalry, with its glories and its vices; on the other side, Equality, with its ardour and its hopes.

Which of these two principles, — Privilege, Equality, — was to govern this Great Republic?

## CHAPTER XXXI.

### Colour.

ONE chance the white man had, and still might have — of living here, in Virginia, also down in Alabama, Mississippi, and the Carolinas, a social and political life apart from his English brother in Pennsylvania, Massachusetts, and Ohio; but the course to be taken by him is one from which it is commonly believed that his pride must revolt, and his taste recoil, — a family alliance with the negro race.

Long before the ugly word miscegenation came into use, and young damsels in ringlets and chignons stood up in public pleading for a mixture of breeds, many sincere, and some serious, men had preached the dogma of a saving quality in the negro blood. Channing had prepared the way for Anna Dickenson. In their flowery prose, the New England teachers had bestowed upon their negro client in the South an emotional nature far above anything that his poor white brother in the North could boast. On the hard and selfish side of his intellect, a white man might be cursed with keener power; the point was moot; but in all that concerned his moral nature, — the religious instincts, the family affections, the social graces — the negro was declared to be a softer, sweeter, and superior being.

He was far more sensitive to signs and dreams, to the voice of birds, to the cries of children, to the heat of noon, to the calm of night. He had a finer ear for song, a quicker relish for the dance. He loved colour with a wiser love. He had a deeper yearning after places; a fresher delight in worship; a livelier sense of the Fatherhood of God. These fancy pictures of the negro — drawn in a New England study, a thousand miles from a rice-field and a cotton plantation — culminated in Uncle Tom.

Many good people in the North had begun to think it would be well for these pale and bilious shadows of the South to marry their sons and daughters to such highly-gifted and emotional creatures, with a view to restoring the strength, and thickening the fibre, of their race. When the War broke out, this feeling spread; as it raged and stormed, this feeling deepened: and now when the War is over, and the South lies prostrate, there is a party in New England, counting women in its ranks, who would be glad, if they could find a way, to marry the whole white population, living south of Richmond, to the blacks. Again and again I have heard men, grave of face and clean of life, declare in public, and to sympathising hearers, that a marriage of white and black would improve the paler stock. In every case these marriages were to happen a long way off. I have met more than one lady who did not shrink from saying that, in her belief, it would be a great improvement for some of the fair damsels of Charleston and of Savannah to wed black husbands. I never met a lady who said it would be well for her own girls to do so.

The War has brought a change in favour of the negro, who is now a petted mortal in the North, to be mentioned as "the coloured gentleman," not as "the damned black rascal" of former times. He rides in the street cars; he has a right to sit by his white brother in a railway; he may enter the same church, and pray in the adjoining pew. Public men make speeches for him, female lecturers expound him. I have heard Captain Anthony, a New England orator, declare that if he wanted to find a good heart in the Southern States, he should look for it under a sable skin; if he wanted to find a good head, he should look for it under woolly hair. That strange thing was said in Kansas, in one of the cleverest speeches I have ever heard.

The fact is, the negro is here the coming man. Parties being nicely poised, the dark men being likely to get votes, they are even now, in view of that heirship, courted, flattered, and cajoled. During the War the negro proved himself a man: — the black and brown lads who rushed into yon fort (now held by Harry Pierman and his imps) made all their fellows men for ever.

Six years ago, as I am told, no lady in Boston, in New York, in Philadelphia, could bear to have a negro servant near her; a black man drank and stank; he was a cheat, a liar, a sot, a thief. I do not find this feeling wholly gone; here and there it may linger for many years; but it is greatly changed; and I have heard very dainty ladies in Boston and

New York, express a liking for the negro as a household help. He is neat and willing; quick with his hand; good-humoured, grateful. Some of his race are handsome, with the grace and style which are held the signs of blood. Here, in Richmond, and at all hotels from New York to Denver, negroes serve at table, shave and dress you, clean your boots, and wait upon your person. In the many hundreds who have been about me, I have never heard one saucy word, never seen one sulky scowl.

One of the negroes whom we saw in Leavenworth was asked whether he would marry and settle, seeing that he had saved a good deal of money. "No, sar, me not marry; no white lady have me; and me not have white woman who marry me for money." On being asked why he could not court and win a woman from his own people, he exclaimed, "Lord, sar! you not think I marry a black nigger wench?" Yet the fellow was a full-blooded negro, black as a piece of coal.

That the negro is fitted, by his humour, by his industry, by his sociality, for a very high form of civil life, may be safely assumed. Some negroes are rich and learned, practise at the bar, preach from the pulpit, strut upon the stage. Many have a great desire to learn and to get on. Here is Eli Brown, head-waiter in the Richmond hotel; a man with a bright eye, a sharp tongue, a quick hand. A few months since he was a slave. He learned to read in secret, and in daily fear of the lash; since he got his freedom, he has learned to write. In this black lad, I have found more sense of right and wrong, of policy and justice, than in half the platform orators of the schools. "Tell me, Eli, do you want a vote?" I said to him in the after-dinner chat, as he stood behind my chair. "Not now, sir," he replied; "I have not read enough yet, and do not understand it all. Sometime I would like to vote, like the others; in twenty or twenty-five years." Is not a man with so much sense fitter for the franchise than a pot-house yelper, who does not know how much he has still to learn?

Last night, I went with Eli round this city; not to see its stores and bars, its singing-rooms, and hells; but bent on a series of peeps into the negro schools. They are mostly up in garrets, or down in vaults; poor rooms, with scant supplies of benches, desks, and books. In some, the teacher is a white; in many he is either a black or half-caste. Old men, young lads, were equally intent on learning in these humble schools; fellows of sixty pottering with the pen, and flat-nosed little urchins tugging at their A B C. All were working with a will; bent on conquering the first great obstacles to knowledge. These men are not waiting for the world to come and cheer them with its grand endowments and its national schools; they have begun the work of emancipating themselves from the thraldom of ignorance and vice. In Richmond only there are forty of these negro schools.

In the front of men inspired by such a spirit, the planters cannot afford to lie still and rust in their ancient pride. Knowledge is power, and the weaker man always goes to the wall. But though the planter may, and must, prepare himself to compete with a new class on his own estate, does it follow that he must mix his blood with that of his former slave?

The feeling of aversion to the negro as an associate, even for a passing moment in a room, a church, a railway carriage, though it may be softening, as the negro grows in freedom, wealth, and culture, is very strong; not only here, in Richmond, where the negro was a chattel, to be bought and sold, starved, beaten, spat on, by his lordly brother; but in the west and north, in Indianapolis, Cincinnati, and Chicago, far away from the sights and sounds of a servile class. Since the War was closed, a negro has a legal right to enter any public vehicle plying in the streets for hire; but, in many cases, he dares not exercise his right. A cabman would not drive him; a conductor would not let him step into a ladies' car. In passing through Ohio, a state in which the coloured folks are numerous, being struck by the absence of all dark faces from the cars, I went forward to the front of our train, and there, between the tender and the luggage van, found a separate pen, filthy beyond words to suggest, in which were a dozen free negroes, going the same road and paying the same fare as myself. "Why do those negroes ride apart — why not travel in the common cars?" I asked the guard. "Well," said he, with a sudden lightning in his eyes, "they have the right; but, damn them, I should like to see them do it. Ugh!" The ugly shudder of the guard recalled a black expression of Big Elk, one of my Cheyenne comforters on the plains. Here, in Virginia, all the railway companies have posted orders to the effect, that when a negro has paid his fare, he may ride in any car he pleases, subject to the common rules; but, gracious heavens! what negro dares to put his feet on the white man's steps? Sam likes his free condition: at times, he may air his liberty offensively under his former master's nose; but he also loves his skin; and in a land where every man carries a revolver, fingering it as freely as in England we should sport with a cigar-case, Sam knows how far he may go, and where he must stop. Habits are not changed by a paper law; and the day of a perfectly free and friendly intercourse between whites and blacks is yet a long way off.

In Massachusetts and Rhode Island, you will hear it said, in favour of miscegenation, that this scheme for blending races and mixing blood is no new method; but one which has long prevailed in Virginia, Carolina, and Alabama. Your teachers tell you that miscegenation is a fact, not a theory, a Southern habit, not a Northern project. They take you into streets, hotels, and barbers' shops; they bid you look at these yellow negroes, some pale as Moors, some white as Spaniards; and they ask you to tell them whence come these Saxon features, these blue grey eyes, these delicate hands? They show you a negress with golden hair. Do such things prove that the white blood will not mingle with the black? Sail to Newport, ride to Saratoga. These idling places swarm with coloured servants; every man, every woman of whom might be put in evidence of the truth. What is seen in Newport, in Saratoga, is also seen at Niagara, at Long Branch, at Lebanon Springs, at every watering-place in this republic. North of the Potomac, it is a rare thing to find a pure African black. Many of your house-servants are half-castes, more still are quadroons and octoroons. Broad traces of either English or Spanish blood may be seen in nearly all; in the colour, in the carriage, in the contour, in the style. This pale white negro, Pete, has the air of a grandee. Eli, my friend here, has the bearing of a judge. Who knows where Pete, where Eli, got that lofty air? In Virginia, in Carolina, the black squat face, with its huge lips, its low forehead, its open nostrils, is seen in every street. It is not a comely face to look on: though the folks who wear this form and hue are not such brutes as they are sometimes called. Many of them are bright and thriving; Harry Pierman is a full-blooded negro. But even in Richmond these coloured people have a large admixture of Saxon blood. Eli Brown is a half-caste; so is Pete; most of these clever lads, our servants, are quadroons. It is certain, therefore, as the New England teachers say, that miscegenation, instead of being a new thing in the South, has been known and practised for many years.

Thus far, however, it has been practised only on one side, — on the male side; and the new plan for mixing the blood of white and black appears to be only a branch of that mighty theory of reform, now agitating and unsettling all society — the theory of equal rights for sex and sex. Hitherto, miscegenation has been open to men, denied to women. Male

Saxon life has long been passing into negro veins; and that shrewd observer, Captain Anthony, who said he should look for a good heart under a sable skin, a good head under woolly hair, gave this strange reason for his faith in negro courage and negro talent — that the best blood of Virginia and Carolina flows in the veins of this coloured race. For ten generations, he asserts, the youth of this English gentry has been given up to negro paramours; nearly all that time the breeding of slaves for the market has been a trade in these Southern parts. No sense of shame, he says, either prevented a father from giving his heir a pretty quadroon for a playmate, or from afterwards selling the fruits of their illicit love. When, according to Captain Anthony, his youth was spent, his heart was sear, and his brain was dull, this heir of a gentle house was married to a white woman, who bore him children and preserved his name. Is it not clear, asked the speaker, that the strength and freshness of that gentle family should be sought for in negro ranks?

Why, the reformer then comes in and asks, if such things can be allowed on one side, why not on the other? If it be right for a man to love a negro mistress, why should it be wrong for a woman to wed a negro husband? Thus it would appear from a review of facts and sentiments, that this sudden and alarming theory of miscegenation is no more than an effort to make free for all that which is now only free for some; an effort to give legal standing, moral sanction, to what is already a habit of the stronger sex.

But among this stronger sex, with the rare exception of a poet here, a philosopher there, this idea of introducing a fashion of love and wedlock among white women and black men excites the wildest rage. Gentlemen sitting at table, sipping soup, picking terapin, will clench their hands and gnaw their lips at any allusion to the subject. Americans are not squeamish as to jokes; but you must not jest in their society about the loves of black men for white women. Merely for paying a compliment where it is thought he should not, a negro would be flogged and tarred and hung. No punishment would be deemed brutal and fierce enough for such a sinner. A friend who knew what he was saying, told me in the western country that he had seen a negro seized by a mob for having insulted a white girl; his offence was that of giving the girl a kiss, with an appearance of aiming at a further freedom; and on the girl screaming for assistance, he was collared by a soldier, a native of Ohio, and dragged into Fort Halleck, where he was cuffed and kicked, tarred and feathered, set on fire, skinned alive, and finally stuck, half-dead, in a firkin, and exposed on the open Plains, until his flesh was eaten away by wolves and hawks.

My friend, who told me this story, a Missourian by birth, a soldier in the War, had no conception that I should be shocked by such details, that I should consider the punishment in excess of the offence, that I should think the Ohio soldier guilty of a grievous crime. In the Western country life is lightly held and lightly taken. No one puts the high value on a drop of blood which we of the elder country set upon it. A white man counts for little — less than for a horse; a black man counts for nothing — less than for a dog. All this I knew; and therefore I could understand my friend.

A time may perhaps come, as poets feign and preachers prophesy, when the negro man and the Saxon woman will be husband and wife; but the day when they can go to church together, for the celebration of their marriage rites, without exciting the wrath, provoking the revenge, of these masculine protectors of white women, is evidently a long way off.

## CHAPTER XXXII.

#### Reconstruction.

In the great contest now going forward in every part of this Republic as to the safest theory of reconstruction, — that is to say, as to the principle and plan on which the New America may be built up — every party seems to have put the Union in its front. Under the dome of yon glorious New Capitol, men from the North and from the South appeared to be equally eloquent and ardent for the flag. All speakers have the word upon their lips, all writers have the symbol in their style. Unity would seem to be, not only the political religion of men in office, but the inspiration of every man who desires to serve his country. No other cry has a chance of being heard. Not to join in this popular demand is to be guilty of a grave offence. "We are all for the Union," said to me a Virginian lady, not an hour ago, "the Union as it was, if we may have it so; our sole desire is to stand where we stood in '61." So far as you can hear in Richmond, this expression would appear to convey the general wish. North of the Potomac, too, the desire to have done with the past five years of trouble and dissension is universal.

In the new elections, every candidate for office has been forced by the public passion, though often against his will, to adopt this watch-cry of the nation for himself and for his friends; while he has found his profit in denouncing his enemies and their partizans as disunionists, — a denunciation which, in the present temper of men, is taken to imply all the worst treacheries and corruptions, present and to come; in fact, to clothe a man with such uncleanness of mind and body as lay in the Hebrew phrase of a whited-wall. Union is a word of grace, of sweetness and of charm. Everybody takes it to himself, everybody claims it for his section. Dis-union, a word so musical in Richmond, Raleigh, New Orleans, not thirty months ago, is now a ban, a stigma, a reproach. Its day is past. Republicans call their Democratic rivals dis-unionists; Democrats describe their Republican adversaries as dis-unionists. Each section writes the word Union on its ticket, and the shout of this common word from the opposite camps is apt to confuse a free and independent elector when he comes to vote.

Even here, in Richmond, the capital of a proud and fallen cause, in which the streets are yet black with fire, around which the fields are yet sick with blood, there is scarcely any other cry among the wise, the moderate, and the hopeful. A few, unquestionably, cling with a passionate warmth to the memory of the past; but every day, as it goes by, is thinning the ranks of these sentimental martyrs. The young, who feel that their life is before them, not behind, are all coming round to a larger and more practical view of facts. They see that the battle has been fought, that the prize for which they struggled has been lost. Slavery is gone. State-rights are gone. The dream of independence is gone. Men who are hopelessly compromised by events — who feel that the victorious states can never again entrust them with political power — may urge on their fellows the merit and the virtue of despair; but the younger men of this nation feel that sullenness and silence will not help them to undo the victories of Sherman, Sheridan, and Grant. Excepting in the society of women — a class of generous and noble, but illogical and impracticable reasoners — not many persons in the South (I am told) regard the prospect of re-union with a free and powerful republic, just awakening, at their instance, to a consciousness of its colossal might, with any other feeling than a proud and eager joy.

Richmond is not, just now, in a mood of much emotion; since she fell into Northern hands her habit has been that of a proud and cold reserve; yet so soon as the pending elections roused in her a little life, her enthusiasm, such as it was, ran wholly in the form of the ancient flag. At a dinner-party given in this city the other day, a politician proposed as a toast, "The fallen flag!" "Hush, gentlemen!" said a son of General Lee, "this sort of thing is past. We have no flag now but the glorious Stars and Stripes, and I will neither fight, nor drink, for any other."

From the tone and temper of such political debate as one hears in Richmond, I see no reason to suspect (with some of the New York papers) that this patriotism of Virginia is the result of either fear or craft; for in my poor judgment, no disaster, however dark, no privation, however keen, could have driven these proud Virginian gentry into pleading for a renewal of friendly relations on other than the usual grounds of political science. The return to wiser feelings on the part of these vanquished soldiers seems to have been the natural consequence of events. The life before them is a new life. Slavery is gone, and the hatreds provoked by slavery are going. Men have to look their fortunes in the face, and it is well that they should do it without suffering their judgment to be warped by the disturbing passions so commonly found on a losing side. How are the planters to maintain their place — not in the Great Republic only, but in Carolina and Virginia? At present they are an aristocracy without a servile class. They have great estates; but they have no capital, no mills, no ships, no labourers. They are burdened with enormous debts. They have scarcely any direct and independent intercourse with foreign nations. Worse than all, they are surrounded, in their fields and in their houses, by a population of inferior race. Does it need any more than a little good sense to perceive that the English gentry in the South may find their best account in a partnership with the English citizens of the North, even though these latter should impose on the repentant prodigals a forgiving kinsman's terms?

The blacks are strong in numbers, clannish in spirit; they are fond of money, and have the virtue to earn and save. Can you prevent the negroes from growing rich, from educating their children at good schools, from aspiring to offices of trust and power? They will rise, both individually and in classes. The day is not far distant when, in states like Alabama and South Carolina, the race may be swift and hard between the black planter and the white. When that day comes, will it not be well for the white man to have gained for himself some support in the power and enterprise of his brother in the North?

In these semi-tropical parts of the Republic a white man faints where the black man thrives. Nature has, therefore, put the white planter at a disadvantage on this southern soil. For a dozen years to come, perhaps more, the negroes, who were only yesterday in chains and poverty, may be sorely tried; for they are rooted to the soil; they have neither trades nor callings; they are ignorant of letters; they have very little money; scarcely any of them have friends. Before them stands a world in which they are free to labour and free to starve. At first, they must be servants in the families, toilers on the plantations, in which they have recently been slaves; yet in some cases the negro has already become a planter on his own account, having gained, in a few months, a supply of tools and a lease of lands.

Take the example of my friend Henry Pierman, a negro, who has planted himself out yonder in Harrison's Fort, in a log-cabin, amidst the reek and stench of the great battle-fields. As no white man would rent such land, the lady who owns it, poorer and less proud than she was in former years, has been glad to let a great patch of forest to Henry. The log-hut has but a single room, and in this one room he lives with his black and comely wife, his four young imps, and a brood of cocks and hens. Harry was a slave, until Grant tore his way through these formidable lines, when he became free by the great act of war which made all his people free. Happily for him, he had been a domestic slave in one of those rich Virginian households in which nobody cared about the laws. One of the young ladies, more for fun than with serious thought, had defied the police and the magistrate by teaching him to read. Her father being the Governor of Virginia, she snapped her pretty fingers at the judge. Harry read the Bible, and became a member of the Baptist church. Like all his brethren, he is keenly alive to religious passion, subject to dreams and voices, one of which had told him, he asserts, while he was yet a youth and a slave, that he would one day become a free man, would marry, would have children, and would rent a farm of his own. Many years went by before his dream came out, but he prayed and waited; in the end he found that this promise of his youth was kept. So soon as the liberating armies entered Richmond, he left his old place, though his master had been kind to him, and wished to keep him as a servant on hire; but the passion to be free was in his veins; voices called him from the city into the fields; and, without money, ploughs, scythes, seed, horses, stock of any kind, with only his black wife to help him, and his three youngsters to feed, he threw himself on the forest land. Last year, his trial-year, was found to be bitter work, but he had put his soul into his task, and he got on. Up early and late, pinching his back and his belly, he was able to send a few onions and tomatoes, a little corn and wood, to market. This produce bought him tools, and paid his rent in kind. By patience he got through the winter months. In the second year his enterprises have extended to a hundred and forty acres, and he has now the help of two other negroes, one of them his wife's father, whom he has lodged in another of these soldiers' huts. One-fourth of his produce pays the rent; the remaining three-fourths he divides into two equal portions, one of which he gives to his negro helpers, the other he retains for himself and wife. Henry is clever, pushing, devout; for his children, if not for himself, he is ambitious. One of his lads is shortly to begin his school-work; at present he must toil upon the farm. "I heard de angel say in my dream," he said to me with simple faith, "dat I bring up my children in de fear of de Lord, and how man bring dem up in fear of de Lord, unless he teach dem to read and write?"

The field of enterprise for working men like Henry Pierman is extremely wide. Two-thirds of the soil of Virginia are still uncleared; indeed this old and lovely state is everywhere rich in mines, in water-ways, in wood and coal, which a splendid and careless people have left to wait and rot. Each year will see the band of negro farmers grow on these Virginian waste lands; and when the coloured people have grown rich and educated, how can they be kept from social and political power? In some states of the South, they are many: in one state, South Carolina, they count more than half the population; so that South Carolina, standing by itself and governed by universal suffrage, would vote itself a negro legislature, perhaps a negro governor. These dark people are growing faster than the pale. In time they will own ships and mines, banks and granaries; and when they have gathered up money and votes, how will the white man be able to hold his easy and safe supremacy in these semi-tropical states unless by union with his white brethren in the North?

Of course, while every hope and every fear may be thus impelling North and South to re-unite, each section may still desire to construct the New America on terms best suited to itself. Deprived by the war of their slaves, laden with debts, both personal and territorial, the Southern planters would like to rejoin the ancient league as equals, if it may be, as more than equals. Under the old constitution they were more than equals, since they voted for themselves and for their slaves; and what they were aforetime they would like to be again.

But Northern statesmen, flushed with their recent glories, have no mind to put back the sword into its sheath, until they shall have fully secured the objects for which they fought; one of which objects is, to prevent, in future, a Charleston planter from exercising in the national councils a larger share of power than falls to the lot of a manufacturer of Boston, a banker of New York. Such larger share of power the Constitution had given to the Charleston planter, on account of his holding property in slaves; representation in the Capitol being based on population; five negroes counting for three free men; and the masters voting, not for themselves only, but for their slaves. The strife of policy rages for the moment wholly around this point.

The two moderate parties, between which the struggle of the coming years will mainly lie, are the Republican and the Democrat. The Republicans, strong in the North, are weak in the South; the Democrats, strong in the South, are weak at the North; but each party has its organisation and its followers in every state of the Republic. They have other points of difference; but the chief contention now dividing them, is as to what guarantees shall be demanded from the rebellious states before they come into Congress and take their chances in the fight for power.

The Republicans say, that all white men in the Union, that is to say, all the voters, should be made equal to each other before the ballot-box; that each man should poll once and for himself only, with no distinction of North or South. The black man they leave out of their account; he is to them as a minor, a woman; having no rights at the poll and in the legislature. This change in the law of voting cannot be made and put into force until the Constitution shall have been first amended. That charter based the power of representation on population, without regard to the number of voters. The negroes counted as people, and their masters got the political profit of their presence on the soil. In the Old America, the planters who exercised this power may have fairly represented the negro mind, so far as negroes had opinions and emotions; but this Old America is gone for ever; the planter can no longer answer for his slave; and his claim by the old law to give this vote on the black man's behalf, must be done away. In future, all white men in the United States must have an equal power at the poll; hence, the Republicans have framed a bill, amending the Constitution so far as to base the representation in Congress not on the number of persons, but on the number of voters. A majority in the new Congress is certain to be of opinion that this bill should pass.

The Democrats assert that any amendment of the Constitution is illegal, revolutionary, needless. They say, and in theory they rightly say, that representation should be based on population; on a great natural fact, easily ascertained, capable of proof; not on a whimsy, a convenience of the day, a mere local act, which may be passed to-day, recalled to-morrow. They clench the doctrine which the moderate section among Republicans profess to have adopted, that a black man, in his present state of ignorance, is not fit to vote; but then they add, that as the black man shall not vote himself, his more liberal and enlightened neighbour, like the electoral classes in a European state, should be allowed to cast his vote into the urn. These Democrats have the great advantage of seeming to stand by the law and constitution, but their reasoning against the constitutional bill is seen to be futile and unsound. President Johnson and his cabinet are of opinion that this Constitutional Amendment should not pass.

Each party finds a certain amount of sympathy in the hostile camp. The Northern Radicals object to the Constitutional Amendment as illegal and unnecessary; asserting, with the Democrats, that representation should be based on natural population, not on the number of legal voters; asserting, with the Republicans, that all white men should have equal rights in the urn; and declaring, in the face of both these parties, that the negro should be allowed to give his vote for himself. In like manner, the Southern moderates, while they hold to many doctrines which the North will not endorse, are not unwilling to unite with them on the terms of equal rights proposed by the Republicans. This party of peace and compromise is perhaps the strongest, numerically, in the South; but the hopes of more fanatical men have been so hotly fanned by President Johnson and his agents, that calm and reasonable counsels have been heard among the old governing classes with a certain stiffness and impatience.

We need not judge these parties with heat and haste. After her losses in the field, the South may easily persuade herself that she has a right to ask for much, and to take whatever advantages she can of the divided counsels of her foes.

## CHAPTER XXXIII.

#### Union.

THE main obstacle, then, to a Union, such as late events have made possible, and the interests of all parties would suggest, is not the temper of either North or South, but the existence of a paper-law, for which every American has been trained to express a veneration almost equal to that which he professes for the Word of God.

If any human effort of the pen is sacred in the eyes of these people it is their Constitution. Indeed, a stranger in the land can hardly comprehend the reverence — sometimes rising into awe — with which brave Virginians, practical Pennsylvanians, bright New Englanders, always speak of their Organic law. Apart from the affection borne to it by a great people, that organic law, from whatever point of view it is regarded, fails to impress a student of politics as being the highest effort of human genius. It is less than a hundred years old, and has none of the halo which comes of time. It was not a growth of the soil and of the English mind, but an exotic, drawn from the foreign and artificial atmosphere of France. On the day of its adoption it was no more than a compromise, and ever since that day it has stood in the way of progress in the United States. The principles embodied in it are in direct antagonism to that splendid document, which often lies by its side in the text-books — the Declaration of Independence; for the Constitution denies that all men are free and equal, and refuses to large classes of the people the pursuit of their own happiness.

Who can forget how often, and with what success, that Constitution has been cited in evidence that the negro slave was not considered by the founders of this Republic as a human being? If all men are pronounced free and equal, by the fact of their birth, it is only too obvious that creatures held in bondage are *not men*. But every one knows that the Declaration of Independence set forth the true and final views of those founders, while the Constitution expressed no more than the political compromises of a day. The very men who signed it wished it to be amended; in the first convulsion which has tried the political fabric of this country, it is found to be the cause of a thousand disasters. It has brought the country to such a stand that years may possibly elapse before the facts which have been accomplished, and which cannot be reversed, can be set in harmonious relation to the paper laws.

While Americans are busy, unmaking and amending their Constitution, may they not fairly put to themselves the question, What is the use of this record? At best, when the letter of a constitution is true in every detail — true to the designs of God in His moral government of men, true to the life and hope of the people in whose name it is drawn up — it is only a definition of facts. It is a thing of the past; a record of what the people have been, and of what they are. But the act of defining is also one of narrowing, limiting, restricting. Why should the life of a great continent be narrowed down to a phrase? How can a progressive country pretend to limit its power of future growth? By what right may a free commonwealth presume to restrain the march of ideas and events? In a despotic state, where men are neither free nor equal, where growth is not expected, where prosperity is not desired, a paper law, unchanging as that of the Medes and Persians, may have reason for existence; for under such a rule the people can never hope to rise into that highest state of being a law unto themselves. In a country like America, a real constitution should be a vital fact, not a piece of paper, and a dubious phrase. England never had a written constitution. How could she have? Her constitution is her life. All that she has ever been, ever done, ever suffered — these are her constitutions, because they are herself. What would she gain by trying to write down this story in a dozen articles? She would gain a set of manacles. No dozen phrases could express the whole of her vitalities. Some of these are obvious, others latent; no one can remember all the past, no one can foresee all the future. Why not be content to let the nation live? Would any sane man think of making a constitution for a garden, of hanging a paper chain on the stems of plants? Yet men in a free soil have wider possibilities of change in them than trees and flowers. Could anybody dream of devising a constitution for sciences like chemistry, astronomy, and physics? Where you have power of growth, you must have order, method, understanding; not a final theory, not an infallible law.

And what are the advantages derived from a Constitution? Are you afraid that people would forget their principles and betray their freedom, unless they were restrained from wandering by these paper notes? That is the common fear. But see what this fear implies, and say whether all that it implies is just. As men cannot wander from their own natures, their own instincts and passions, you have to assume that your Constitution has a life apart from that of your people; that it is a political fiction, not a moral and social truth. If the Constitution exists in the blood and brain of this bright and tenacious people — if it be the genuine product of what they have done, of what they are — you need not fear its being forgotten and betrayed. If it is an alien statute, what right have you to force it upon them?

In the present state of feeling with respect to the Constitution, I do not think that anybody would be heard with patience who should propose to set the people free, by putting it to a decent end. The time for such a work may come. At present no one dreams of doing more than amending a defective instrument in several places; so as to cast away some of the very worst articles inserted in it by the slave proprietors. Only the radicals propose to bring t into harmony with the Declaration of Independence. But while the political doctors are at work

upon it, may it not be worth their while to consider
— Whether it would not be better to confine their
task to cutting away the obnoxious parts? Why not
open the Constitution by removing its restrictions?
Why add to a document which they admit to be
defective? They know that if this paper barrier
had not stood in their way, the differences between
North and South would have ended with the defeat
of Lee. Why then prepare fresh difficulties for their
children, by adding new compromises to the organic
statutes?

In a few years North and South will be one
again; state rights will have been forgotten, and the
negro will have found his place. A free Republic
cannot hope to enjoy the repose of a despotic state;
to combine the repose of Pekin with the movement
of San Francisco, the order of Miako with the
vitality of New York. Ebb and flow may be predicted of the future; at one time public thought will
be found ebbing towards separation, personality, and
freedom; another time it will be found flowing again
towards union, brotherhood, and empire; but the
tides of sentiment may be expected to roll from East
to West, from West to East, without provoking a
second wreck. That article left uncertain in the
Constitution, as to the power of any one state to
part from its fellows without their leave, has been
now defined by facts. War on that question will
not come again; but heats will come, passions will
be roused, and orators will take the field, even
though the sword may not again be drawn; one
side in the fray waxing eloquent on the rights of

man, the other side on the power of states. Who shall say which fury burns with the whiter rage? One party will take its stand on personal freedom, the other will take its stand on national strength. These forces are immortal. One age will fight for independence, a second will fight for empire, just as either the Saxon or the Latin spirit shall happen to prevail. When these two powers are in poise and balance, then, and then only, will the republic enjoy the highest share of freedom with the widest share of power.

When the armies came into collision after the fall of Fort Sumter, the true banner of the war was raised, and the battle was accepted on a broader ground. The issue of the fight was then, — What principle shall the Great Republic write upon her flag? Shall her society be founded on the principles of Chivalry, or on the principles of Equality? Shall industry be branded as ignoble? Shall the New America be a slave empire or a free commonwealth?

Under these walls of Richmond the battle of that principle was fairly fought; with a skill, a pride, a valour, on either side to recall the charges at Naseby and at Marston Moor; but the Cavaliers went down, and the Middle Ages then lost their final field.

When the reign of that martial and seceding spirit came to its close in the midst of rout and fire, the milder spirit of Unity and peace, which had only slept in the heart of these American hosts, came up to the front. A new order was commenced; not in much strength at first; not without fears and failings; yet the reign of a nobler sentiment was opened, and every eye can see how far it is daily gaining in strength and favour; even though it has to contend against craft and passion more fatal than the sword. Years may elapse before this Union sentiment in the South is strong with all the riches of its strength; but the heralds have blown their horns, and the soldiers have raised their flag. Fulness of life must come with time; enough for the hour that the desire for Unity has been born afresh.

Yes; here in Richmond, among these gallant swordsmen of the South, on whom the war has fallen with its deadliest weight — men broken in their fortunes, widowed in their affections — many admit, and some proclaim, that they have made a surprising change of front. They are still the same men as before the war, but they have wheeled about and set their faces another way. Some, it has been said, cannot make this change; they had their part in the past, and with the past they fell. Men whose last act was to burn this city, when they fled, leaving these blackened walls, these broken columns, these empty thoroughfares, as a message, a memorial of their despair, may think they have the right to be heard, and to be considered in these southern cities; but it is coming to be understood that if the past is theirs, for weal and woe, there is a future before the world in which they can have no share. The victors have set their mark upon them, so that they shall fill no further office of command. Their friends may grieve over this exclusion; but the nation has to live; and the rank and file of the

South will not punish itself for ever, even for the sake of those who, in their enthusiasm, may have misled it into death. In fact, the tide has turned; the same sea rolls and swells; but the ebb of separation has become the tide of Union.

Though late, a goodly number of these planters see that their fiery haste, their brave impatience, their impetuous valour, had urged them on too fast and far; so fast, that in their rage for liberty they would have murdered law; so far, that in their quest of independence they would have sacrificed empire. In their passion to be free they had forgotten the saving power and virtue which belong to order, balance, equipoise of powers. To gain their darling wish — the right to stand alone — they would have rent society to shreds, and put the world back in its course a thousand years. They see their error now, and would undo their work; so far as such a deed can ever be undone. A few still hug their pride and weakness; reading no promise in the skies; and courting the fate of Poland for the South. Others among them may be silent: scanning these crumbling streets, yon Yankee sentinels, those shouting negroes in the lane, with bitter smile; but time is doing upon these sad spirits its healing work. They feel that, having lost their cause, they must yield to nature: — an Anglo-Saxon cannot sink into a Pole.

I do not mean to say that here, in Richmond, the banner of Robert Lee is trodden in the mire: it is not; neither should it be, since that banner gleamed only over men who had armed to defend a cause in which they found much glory and felt no shame. I only say that the banner of Lee has been rolled to its staff, and put away among things of the past, with much of the chivalric error, the romantic passion, of the South laid up and smoothed among its folds. Good sense, if not fraternal love, has been restored to these gallant people; who see well enough that the past is past, that rage is vain, that the fight is over, that a place in the country may yet be won. At present they are nothing; less than the mean whites; less than their own negroes. The situation cannot last. "Most of our young," said a Virginian to me just now, "are in favour of going in;" that is to say, of compromising the dispute, and taking their seats in Congress: "they do not like seeming to desert their old generals, but they want to live; and they won't stand out for ever." These younger men, against whom the victors entertain no grudge, have nearly forgotten the past five years. Youth keeps its eyes in front, and there it sees nothing but the flag.

Hence it comes that in these very streets of Richmond, men who were yesterday on horseback, charging for the Confederate device, are now heard whispering of the Stars and Stripes, with a regret not feigned, an affection not put on. "Our grand mishap," said to me a Georgian soldier, not an hour ago, "was our change of flag; we should have kept the old silk; we should have gone out boldly for the Union; we should have put yon Yankees on the outer side; we should have taken our ground on the Constitution, making our enemies the Seceders; then, we should have won the fight, for all the West would have been with us; and, instead of stamping about these blackened walls to-day, we should have had our piquets at Niagara, our sentries at Fanieul Hall." Perhaps he is right. But is not this regret of the Georgian an after-stroke? Was any such thought as that of holding on by the old flag, of preserving the Great Republic, to be found in the Southern States when the war came down? The rage was then for separation. If wiser thoughts have come, have they not come by trial, in the wake of strife and loss? Those who now put their faith in Union, who look to the Capitol, to the White House for safety, held in those years by another doctrine; putting their trust in freedom, independence, personality. That dogma failed them; isolation would not work; personality would not pay. Law and policy were against them; the instincts of society were too strong for them. They fought for their scheme of separation; they failed; and, failing, lost both prize and stake; all that for which they had tempted fortune, nearly all that which they had put upon the die.

Happily for the world, they failed and lost; failed by a law of nature, lost by an ordinance of Heaven. No calamity in politics could have equalled the success of a slave-empire, founded on the ruin of a strong republic. All free nations would have felt it, all honest men would have suffered from it; but even with their mistaken cause, their retrograde policy, their separatist banner, what a fight they made! Men who can perish gloriously for their faith —

however false that faith may be — will always seize the imagination, hold the affections of a gallant race. Fighting for a weak and failing cause, these planters of Virginia, of Alabama, of Mississippi, rode into battle as they would have hurried to a feast; and many a man who wished them no profit in their raid and fray, could not help riding, as it were, in line with their foaming front, dashing with them into action, following their fiery course, with a flashing eye and a bounding pulse. Courage is electric. You caught the light from Jackson's sword, you flushed and panted after Stuart's plume. Their sin was not more striking than their valour. Loyal to their false gods, to their obsolete creed, they proved their personal honour by their deeds; these lords of every luxury under heaven, striving with hunger and with disease, and laying down their luxurious lives in ditch and breach. All round these walls, in sandy rifts, under forest leaves, and by lonely pools, lie the bones of young men, of old men, who were once the pride, the strength of a thousand happy Anglo-Saxon homes. Would that their sin could be covered up with a little sand!

Out on yon lovely slope of hill, from the brow of which the reddening woods and winding waters of beautiful Virginia gladden the eyes of men for leagues and leagues, the pious North has gathered into many beds, under many white stones, the ashes of her illustrious dead; of youths who came down from their farms in Ohio, from their mills in Vermont, from their schools in Massachusetts; the thew, the nerve, the brain of this great family of free-men;

who came down, singing their hymns and allelujahs; giving up ease, and peace, and love, and study, to save their country from division, from civil war, from political death. Singing their hymns, they fainted by the way-side; shouting their allelujahs, they were stricken in the trench and in the field. New England gave its best and bravest to that slope. I know a street in Boston from every house in which death has taken spoil; in the houses of poet and teacher, I have seen Rachel mourning with a proud joy for the sons who will never come back to her again. These heroes sleep on the hill-side, in the city which defied and slew them; they have entered it as conquerors at last; and here they will keep their silent watch, the sentinels of a bright and holy cause. All glory to them, now and for evermore!

Out, too, in yon swamps and wastes, by the deserted breastwork, by the fallen fort, by the rank river margin, lie the ashes of a broken and ruined host; of young men, of old warriors, who rode up from the cotton lands of Louisiana, from the country-houses of Georgia, from the rice-fields of Carolina, to fight for a cause in which they had learned to feel their right; soldiers as honest, as brave, and proud as any of their stronger and keener foes. But the strong were right, and the right were strong; and the weaker side went down in their fierce embrace. They fell together; their duty done, their passion spent. Many a tender office, many a solemn greeting, passed between these falling brothers, who spoke the same tongue, who muttered the same prayer, who owned one country and one God. They died on the same field, and whitened on the same earth. Still, here and there, some pious hand picks up their bones together, just as the warriors fell in battle, and laying them side by side, leaves the two brothers who had come to strife, victor and vanquished, unionist and seceder, to sleep the long sleep in a common bed.

Would it were always thus! would that the pious North, noble in its charity as in its valour, would condone the past! The dead are past offending any more, and the pious searcher, in presence of a soldier's dust, should ask no question of state and party, but lay the erring prodigal by his brother's side. Yon sunny Richmond slope, on which the setting sun appears to linger, tipping with pink the fair white stones, should be for North and South alike a place of rest, a sign of the New America; an imperishable proof of their reconciliation, no less than an everlasting record of their strife.

**THE END.**

www.ingramcontent.com/pod-product-compliance
Lightning Source LLC
Chambersburg PA
CBHW030119240426
43673CB00041B/1329